English Missions!

Starter

Robert Hickling
Misato Usukura

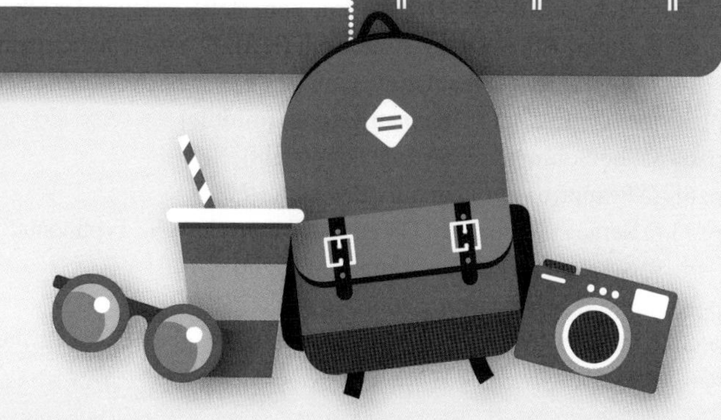

KINSEIDO

Kinseido Publishing Co., Ltd.
3-21 Kanda Jimbo-cho, Chiyoda-ku,
Tokyo 101-0051, Japan

Copyright © 2019 by Robert Hickling
Misato Usukura

All rights reserved. No part of this publication may be reproduced, stored in a retrieval system, or transmitted, in any form or by any means, electronic, mechanical, photocopying, recording or otherwise, without the prior permission of the publisher.

First published 2019 by Kinseido Publishing Co., Ltd.

Design Nampoosha Co., Ltd.
Illustrations Toru Igarashi

Photos
p. 18 © Sstoll850 | Dreamstime.com (left)
p. 23 © Hel080808 | Dreamstime.com (right)
p. 33 © Msghita | Dreamstime.com (middle), © Stevehymon | Dreamstime.com (right)
p. 38 © Helena Bilkova | Dreamstime.com (left), © Bounder32h | Dreamstime.com (middle)
p. 48 © Junior Braz | Dreamstime.com (left), © Nickjene | Dreamstime.com (middle)
© Jon Bilous | Dreamstime.com (right)
p. 58 © Wangkun Jia | Dreamstime.com (middle)
p. 63 © Joe Sohm | Dreamstime.com (right)
p. 68 © Peanutroaster | Dreamstime.com (left)
p. 73 © Sergey Chernyaev | Dreamstime.com (left), © Typhoonski | Dreamstime.com (middle)
© Sergio Vila | Dreamstime.com (right)
p. 83 © Pxlxl | Dreamstime.com (right)
p. 88 © Ackphoto | Dreamstime.com (left), © Rgbe | Dreamstime.com (right)

音声ファイル無料ダウンロード

https://www.kinsei-do.co.jp/download/4070

この教科書で DL 00 の表示がある箇所の音声は、上記 URL または QR コードにて無料でダウンロードできます。自習用音声としてご活用ください。

- ▶ PC からのダウンロードをお勧めします。スマートフォンなどでダウンロードされる場合は、**ダウンロード前に「解凍アプリ」をインストール**してください。
- ▶ URL は、**検索ボックスではなくアドレスバー (URL 表示欄)** に入力してください。
- ▶ お使いのネットワーク環境によっては、ダウンロードできない場合があります。

CD 00 左記の表示がある箇所の音声は、教室用 CD（Class Audio CD）に収録されています。

はしがき

*English Missions! Starter*は４技能をバランスよく使いながら英語の基礎を学ぶことができる教科書です。登場するのは、旅行好きの大学生・エミとリョウ。この２人がアメリカとカナダの都市を旅し、様々な人との出会いを通して多くの体験を重ねていく様子を追いかけながら、日常生活や旅先で使う英語表現や基本的な文法事項を学ぶだけでなく、アメリカやカナダの歴史や文化についても触れることができます。全15ユニットあり、各ユニットは５ページで構成されています。各ユニットの構成は次のようになっています。

Mission !

各ユニットには、２つのMission!が設定されています。Mission!をクリアすることを目指して学びましょう。

Getting Ready

Ⓐ イラスト中から、４つの単語・語句に合うものを選びます。（２～３分）

Ⓑ イラストを見ながら４つの短い英文を聞いて、T／F問題に答えます。なお、４つの英文中には、Ⓐで学んだ単語・語句が使われています。（５分）

Conversation

Ⓐ 会話を聞いて、内容に関する選択肢式の問題に答えます。（５分）

Ⓑ もう一度会話を聞いて、会話中の空所を埋めます。（10分）

Mission ! 1

会話に登場したセリフの音声を聞いた後で、自分でも言ってみる活動です。セリフには、旅行や日常生活で使える会話表現が盛り込まれていますので、何回も練習して覚えるようにしましょう。（２～３分）

Breaking Down the Grammar

ターゲットとなる文法項目を、豊富な例文と簡潔な日本語の説明で学びます。冒頭には「基本例文」が示されていますので、まずはこの文を覚えましょう。（15分）

Grammar Checking

Ⓐ 選択肢式の文法練習問題（８問）です。(10分)

Ⓑ 文法項目への理解を確かにするための練習問題です。ここでは、文の並べ替えや書き換え、穴埋め問題など、文法項目によって問題形式に変化をつけています。(10分)

Reading

２人の登場人物がつけている旅行日記（Travelog）を読んで、日記で紹介されている順に３枚の写真に番号を振る活動です。アメリカ、カナダの様々な場所について、旅行感覚で学ぶことができます。(10分)

Mission ! 2

最後に、各ユニットで学んだ文法項目を使って、短い会話形式で自分自身について書いてみる活動にチャレンジします。完成した会話を使って、ペアで会話練習を行ってもよいでしょう。会話例を収録した音声も用意されています。(10分)

この他、巻末には付録として会話表現 & 基本例文一覧（各Mission! 1で取り上げた表現とBreaking Down the Grammarの基本例文のリスト）、不規則変化動詞一覧も用意しました。予習・復習にぜひご活用ください。

最後に、本書の作成にあたり、金星堂の皆様から多くのご助言・ご支援をいただいただけでなく、多大なご尽力を賜りました。この場をお借りしてお礼申し上げます。

著者一同

本書はCheckLink（チェックリンク）対応テキストです。

CheckLinkのアイコンが表示されている設問は、CheckLinkに対応しています。

CheckLinkを使用しなくても従来通りの授業ができますが、特色をご理解いただき、授業活性化のためにぜひご活用ください。

CheckLinkの特色について

大掛かりで複雑な従来のe-learningシステムとは異なり、CheckLinkのシステムは大きな特色として次の３点が挙げられます。

1. これまで行われてきた教科書を使った授業展開に大幅な変化を加えることなく、専門的な知識なしにデジタル学習環境を導入することができる。
2. PC教室やCALL教室といった最新の機器が導入された教室に限定されることなく、普通教室を使用した授業でもデジタル学習環境を導入することができる。
3. 授業中での使用に特化し、教師・学習者双方のモチベーション・集中力をアップさせ、授業自体を活性化することができる。

▶教科書を使用した授業に「デジタル学習環境」を導入できる

本システムでは、学習者は教科書のCheckLinkのアイコンが表示されている設問にPCやスマートフォン、携帯電話端末からインターネットを通して解答します。そして教師は、授業中にリアルタイムで解答結果を把握し、正解率などに応じて有効な解説を行うことができるようになっています。教科書自体は従来と何ら変わりはありません。解答の手段としてCheckLinkを使用しない場合でも、従来通りの教科書として使用して授業を行うことも、もちろん可能です。

▶教室環境を選ばない

従来の多機能なe-learning教材のように学習者側の画面に多くの機能を持たせることはせず、「解答する」ことに機能を特化しました。PCだけでなく、一部タブレット端末やスマートフォン、携帯電話端末からの解答も可能です。したがって、PC教室やCALL教室といった大掛かりな教室は必要としません。普通教室でもCheckLinkを用いた授業が可能です。教師はPCだけでなく、一部タブレット端末やスマートフォンからも解答結果の確認をすることができます。

▶授業を活性化するための支援システム

本システムは予習や復習のツールとしてではなく、授業中に活用されることで真価を発揮する仕組みになっています。CheckLinkというデジタル学習環境を通じ、教師と学習者双方が授業中に解答状況などの様々な情報を共有することで、学習者はやる気を持って解答し、教師は解答状況に応じて効果的な解説を行う、という好循環を生み出します。CheckLinkは、普段の授業をより活力のあるものへと変えていきます。

上記３つの大きな特色以外にも、掲示板などの授業中に活用できる機能を用意しています。従来通りの教科書としても使用はできますが、ぜひCheckLinkの機能をご理解いただき、普段の授業をより活性化されたものにしていくためにご活用ください。

CheckLink の使い方

CheckLink は、PC や一部タブレット端末、スマートフォン、携帯電話端末を用いて、この教科書の CheckLink のアイコン表示のある設問に解答するシステムです。

・初めてCheckLinkを使う場合、以下の要領で**「学習者登録」**と**「教科書登録」**を行います。

・一度登録を済ませれば、あとは毎回**「ログイン画面」**から入るだけです。CheckLinkを使う教科書が増えたときだけ、改めて**「教科書登録」を行ってください。**

CheckLink URL

https://checklink.kinsei-do.co.jp/student/

QRコードの読み取りができる端末の場合はこちらから ▶▶▶

ご注意ください! 上記URLは**「検索ボックス」**でなく**「アドレスバー(URL表示欄)」**に入力してください。

▶学習者登録

①上記URLにアクセスすると、右のページが表示されます。学校名を入力し「ログイン画面へ」をクリックしてください。
PCの場合は「PC用はこちら」をクリックしてPC用ページを表示します。同様に学校名を入力し「ログイン画面へ」をクリックしてください。

②ログイン画面が表示されたら**「初めての方はこちら」**をクリックし「学習者登録画面」に入ります。

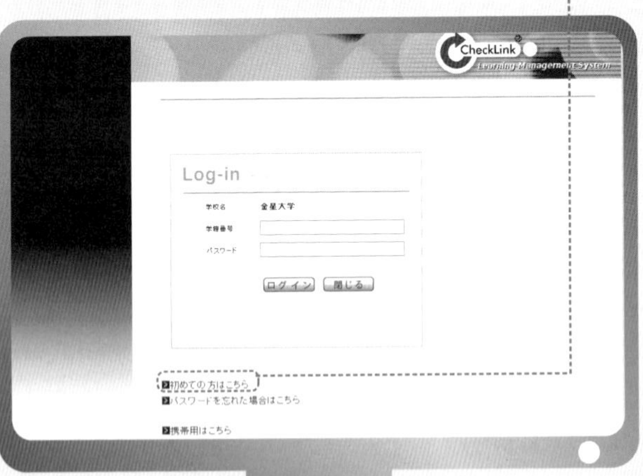

③自分の学籍番号、氏名、メールアドレス(学校のメールなど**PCメールを推奨**)を入力し、次に**任意のパスワード**を8桁以上20桁未満(半角英数字)で入力します。なお、学籍番号はパスワードとして使用することはできません。

④「パスワード確認」は、❸で入力したパスワードと同じものを入力します。

⑤最後に「登録」ボタンをクリックして登録は完了です。次回からは、「ログイン画面」から学籍番号とパスワードを入力してログインしてください。

CheckLink®

▶教科書登録

①ログイン後、メニュー画面から「教科書登録」を選び（PCの場合はその後「新規登録」ボタンをクリック）、「教科書登録」画面を開きます。

②教科書と受講する授業を登録します。
教科書の最終ページにある、**教科書固有番号**のシールをはがし、印字された**16桁の数字とアルファベット**を入力します。

③授業を担当される先生から連絡された**11桁の授業ID**を入力します。

④最後に「登録」ボタンをクリックして登録は完了です。

⑤実際に使用する際は「教科書一覧」（PCの場合は「教科書選択画面」）の該当する教科書名をクリックすると、「問題解答」の画面が表示されます。

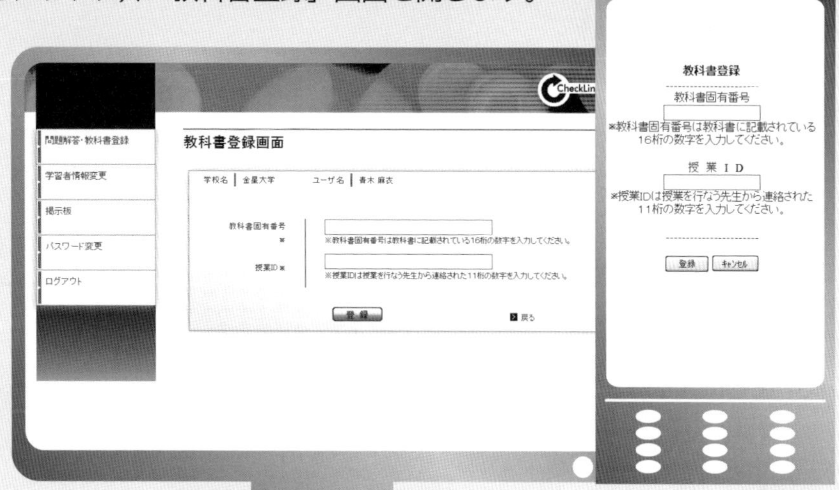

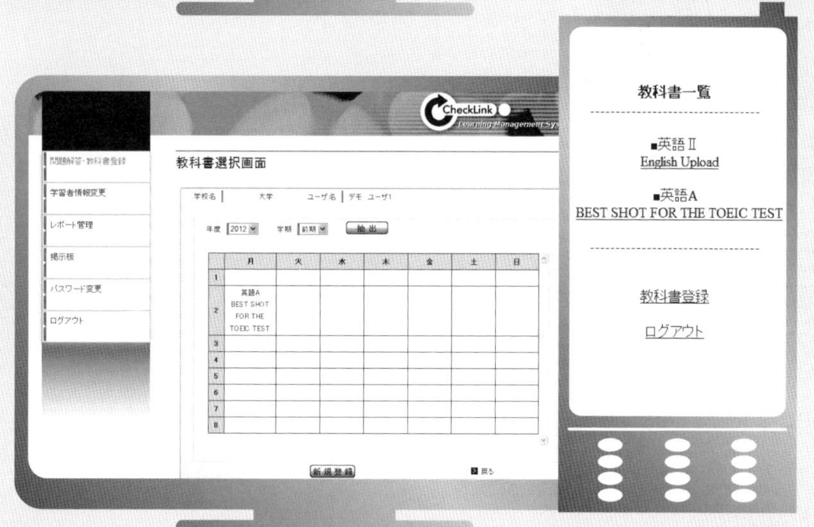

▶問題解答

①問題は教科書を見ながら解答します。この教科書のCheckLinkのアイコン表示のある設問に解答できます。

②問題が表示されたら選択肢を選びます。

③表示されている問題に解答した後、「解答」ボタンをクリックすると解答が登録されます。

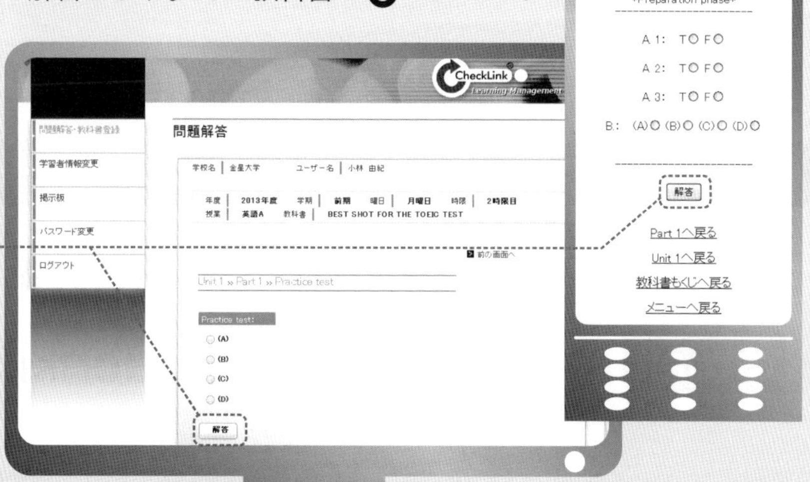

▶CheckLink 推奨環境

PC

推奨 OS
- Windows 7, 10 以降
- MacOS X 以降

推奨ブラウザ
- Internet Explorer 8.0 以上
- Firefox 40.0 以上
- Google Chrome 50 以上
- Safari

携帯電話・スマートフォン

- 3G 以降の携帯電話（docomo, au, softbank）
- iPhone, iPad（iOS9 ～）
- Android OS スマートフォン、タブレット

・最新の推奨環境についてはウェブサイトをご確認ください。
・上記の推奨環境を満たしている場合でも、機種によってはご利用いただけない場合もあります。また、推奨環境は技術動向等により変更される場合があります。

▶CheckLink 開発

CheckLink は奥田裕司 福岡大学教授、正興 IT ソリューション株式会社、株式会社金星堂によって共同開発されました。

CheckLink は株式会社金星堂の登録商標です。

CheckLink の使い方に関するお問い合わせは…

正興 IT ソリューション株式会社　CheckLink 係

e-mail　checklink@seiko-denki.co.jp

English Missions! 

Table of Contents

People & Places

この教科書に登場する人や場所を紹介します。

スズキ・エミ（ Emi Suzuki ）

食べることが大好きで、ちょっとおっちょこちょいの大学生。
新しいことにはどんどん挑戦する、チャレンジ精神の持ち主。
カナダのさまざまな街を巡り、おいしいものを食べ尽くす予定。

Vancouver, Victoria, Canadian Rockies, Toronto, Ottawa, Quebec, P.E.I.

ハシモト・リョウ（ Ryo Hashimoto ）

ジャズが大好きで、夢はプロのベース奏者になること。
初の海外旅行で、アメリカ横断に挑戦する強者。
ちょっと惚れっぽいところがある。

主な旅先

San Francisco, Los Angeles, Grand Canyon, Houston, New Orleans, Miami, New York City

▶ エミとはリョウは同じ大学の友達で、旅の最後に、２人はある場所で落ち合うことになっています。さて、その場所とは…？？

Map of Canada & U.S.A.

各ユニットで２人が訪れる場所を探してみましょう！

Pre-unit

このユニットでは英語の基本語順を勉強します。日本語では「私たちは英語を勉強します」のように「～は」「～を」といった助詞を使いますが、英語には助詞がなくWe study English.のように語句を並べて文を作ります。語順が変わると意味も変わります。

● **英語の基本語順**：英語では主語の次に動詞が来ます。

（例）

誰が（主語）	どうする（動詞）	何を	意味
We	play	basketball.	私はバスケットボールをプレーします。

Check!

Ⓐ 語順に注意して、次の２つの英文の意味を書きましょう。

1. I love sports.

____

2. My grandfather grows vegetables. grow「～を育てる」

____

Ⓑ（　　）内の語句を並べ替えて英文を作りましょう。

1. 私はお金が必要です。(money / need / I)

____

2. たくさんの観光客がこの街を訪れます。(this town / many tourists / visit)

____

● 基本語順＋追加情報

（例）

誰が（主語）	どうする（動詞）	何を	追加情報	意味
We	study	English	after school.	私たちは放課後に英語を勉強します。

Check!

A 語順に注意して、次の２つの英文の意味を書きましょう。

1. My brother takes dance lessons on Friday evenings.

____

2. I eat lunch with my friends at the cafeteria.

____

B（　　）内の語句を並べ替えて英文を作りましょう。

1. 私は毎日中国語を勉強します。(study / every day / I / Chinese)

____

2. 私の父は大学で空手を教えています。(at university / karate / my father / teaches)

____

3. ケンとミキは毎週末に映画を観ます。
(on weekends / Ken and Miki / movies / watch)

____

Welcome to Vancouver

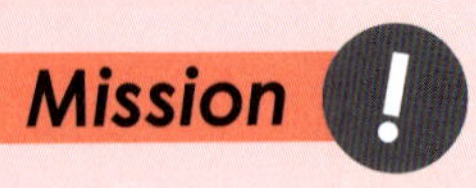

- ホテルにチェックインしよう
- be動詞を使った英文に慣れよう

Getting Ready

エミ (Emi) は、カナダで最初のホテルに到着しました。

A 1～4を表すイラストを上のa～dから選びましょう。

CheckLink DL 02 CD 02

1. guest (　　)　**2.** clerk (　　)　**3.** front desk (　　)　**4.** suitcase (　　)

B イラストを見ながら1～4の英文を聞きましょう。イラストと合っていればT、合っていなければFを選びましょう。

CheckLink DL 03 CD 03

1. T / F　**2.** T / F　**3.** T / F　**4.** T / F

Conversation ● *Is Emi a Chicken?*

ホテルに到着したエミは、フロント係と話をしています。

A 会話を聞いて、聞き取った内容と合っているほうの選択肢を選びましょう。

CheckLink DL 04 CD 04

1. Emi is in (**a.** Vancouver **b.** New York).
2. Emi's last name is (**a.** Suzuki **b.** Sasaki).
3. Emi's reservation is for (**a.** tonight **b.** tomorrow night).
4. The hotel (**a.** is **b.** isn't) full.

B もう一度会話を聞いて、空所を埋めましょう。

Emi: Hello, ([1]) Emi. Umm…

Clerk: Welcome to Vancouver. ([2]) you here to check in, Emi?

Emi: Chicken Emi?

Clerk: No, not chicken — *check in*.

Emi: Oh! Ha ha ha! Yes, **I'm here to check in.**

Clerk: Great. What's your last name — your family name?

Emi: ([3]) Suzuki.

Clerk: Su – zu – ki. …Oh, your reservation ([4]) for tomorrow night.

Emi: Really? ([5]) you sure?

Clerk: Yes, but it's OK. We ([6]) busy tonight.

Emi: Oh, good!

Mission ! 1. セリフを言ってみよう！

音声を聞いて、下のセリフを確認しましょう。その後で、前のページのイラストを見ながら吹き出しのセリフを言ってみましょう。 DL 05 CD 05

"I'm here to check in."

check inは、「チェッキン」のように音がつながります。音のつながりに注意しながら発音しましょう。

Breaking Down the Grammar

Vancouver **is** a beautiful city.
バンクーバーは美しい街です。

●be 動詞は、主語となる人や物の状態や性質を表します。主語に合わせて形が変わり、「主語＋ be 動詞」の組み合わせの後には、主語を説明する様々なことばが続きます。

組み合わせ 「主語（誰が）＋be 動詞」		主語を説明することば 「どうだ」	意味
I	**am**	from Hakodate.	私は函館出身です。
You	**are**	a quiet person.	あなたはおとなしい人です。
He / She / It	**is**	in the kitchen.	彼/彼女/それはキッチンにいます（あります）。
We / You（複数） They	**are**	university students.	私たち/あなたたち/彼らは大学生です。

●否定文を作るときは「主語＋ be 動詞」の後ろに not をつけます。疑問文を作るときは be 動詞と主語の順番を入れ替えます。

David **is not** [**isn't**] a shy person. デービッドは恥ずかしがり屋ではありません。
Are you a member of the basketball team? あなたはバスケットボール部の部員ですか。

●過去形は、主語が I / He / She / It のときは was を、We / You / They のときは were を使います。

It **was** sunny yesterday. 昨日は晴れでした。
The boys **were** members of a rock band.
その少年たちはロックバンドのメンバーでした。

Grammar Checking

A (　　) 内から正しいほうの選択肢を選び、文を完成させましょう。 CheckLink

1. Emi (**a.** is **b.** are) in Canada now.
2. The stores (**a.** isn't **b.** aren't) open today.
3. (**a.** Are **b.** Is) there a post office near here?
4. It (**a.** is **b.** was) really hot yesterday.
5. Karen and I (**a.** are **b.** was) best friends.
6. The vegetables (**a.** wasn't **b.** weren't) very fresh.
7. (**a.** Was **b.** Were) you and Tony at the game?
8. The rooms in this hotel (**a.** is **b.** are) very clean.

B (　　) 内の語句を並べ替えて、日本語に合う文を作りましょう。

1. (teacher / Mr. Brown / a / is) ブラウンさんは先生です。

______________________________.

2. (from / they / aren't / Japan) 彼らは日本出身ではありません。

______________________________.

3. (interesting / was / movie / the / very) その映画はとてもおもしろかったです。

______________________________.

4. (library / Joe / the / in / wasn't) ジョーは図書館にいませんでした。

______________________________.

5. (university / a / are / student / you) あなたは大学生ですか。

______________________________?

Reading ● *Travelog — Vancouver*

エミの旅行日記を読み、紹介されている順に写真a～cに番号を振りましょう。

CheckLink　DL 06　CD 06

I'm in Vancouver. It's a beautiful city between the ocean and mountains. Stanley Park is a big park — with totem poles! Gastown is in the old part of Vancouver, near Chinatown. It's famous for its steam clock. The bridge is 70 meters above the Capilano River. It's safe, but a little scary!

Note: steam「蒸気の」

a. (　　)

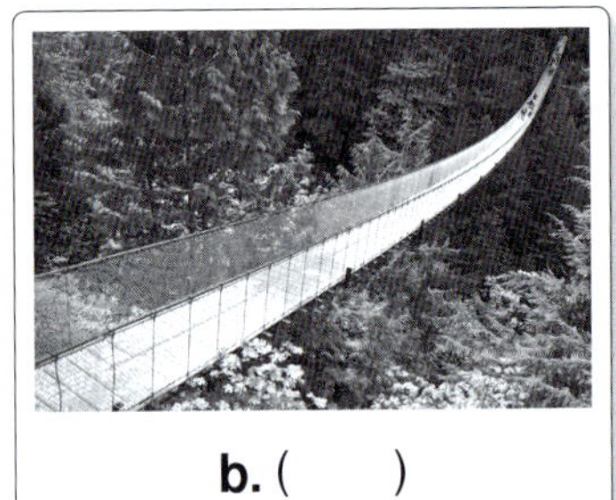
b. (　　)

c. (　　)

Mission ! 2. あなた自身について書いてみよう！

Bのセリフの空所にあなた自身の情報を書き込んで、会話を完成させましょう。
(　　) には be 動詞を使いましょう。

DL 07　CD 07

A: Hi, I'm Jack. What's your name?

B: My name (　　　　) ________________.

A: What's your last name?

B: My last name (　　　　) ________________.

A: Are you from Vancouver?

B: No, (　　　　) not. (　　　　) from ________________.

Unit 2 Ryo Loves San Francisco

Mission !
- 行きたい場所を伝えよう
- 一般動詞の現在形を使った英文に慣れよう

Getting Ready

リョウ（Ryo）は、アメリカのサンフランシスコ国際空港に到着しました。

A 1～4を表すイラストを上のa～dから選びましょう。

CheckLink　DL 08　CD 08

1. information assistant　(　　)　　**3.** souvenir　(　　)

2. backpack　(　　)　　**4.** vending machine　(　　)

B イラストを見ながら1～4の英文を聞きましょう。イラストと合っていればT、合っていなければFを選びましょう。

CheckLink　DL 09　CD 09

1. T / F　　**2.** T / F　　**3.** T / F　　**4.** T / F

Conversation ● *Enjoy Your Stay*

空港のインフォメーションデスクにて、リョウは聞きたいことがあるようです。

A 会話を聞いて、聞き取った内容と合っているほうの選択肢を選びましょう。

CheckLink DL 10 CD 10

1. Ryo (**a.** needs **b.** doesn't need) help.
2. A train runs every (**a.** 15 **b.** 50) minutes.
3. The train ride is (**a.** half an hour **b.** an hour and a half).
4. The lady tells Ryo to take (**a.** an elevator **b.** an escalator).

B もう一度会話を聞いて、空所を埋めましょう。

Information Assistant (IA): Hello. ([1]) you need some help?

Ryo: Yes, **I want to go downtown.** Is there a train?

IA: Yes, a train ([2]) every 15 minutes.

Ryo: Fifty minutes?!

IA: No, not fifty minutes, fifteen minutes. Fif-*teen*.

Ryo: Oh, good! ([3]) it take long?

IA: No, it ([4]) downtown in 30 minutes.

Ryo: Thirty minutes. Great! And the station is…?

IA: Just take the escalator and ([5]) the signs.

Ryo: OK. Thank you very much!

IA: You're welcome. ([6]) your stay.

Mission ! 1. セリフを言ってみよう！

音声を聞いて、下のセリフを確認しましょう。その後で、前のページのイラストを見ながら吹き出しのセリフを言ってみましょう。 DL 11 CD 11

“*I want to go downtown.*”

「～へ行く」と言うときはgo to ~ と表現することが多いですが、「繁華街（街の中心）に行く」と言うときはgo downtownと表現し、toは使いません。

Breaking Down the Grammar　● 一般動詞の現在形

I **work** in San Francisco.
私はサンフランシスコで働いています。

● 一般動詞は、主語となる人や物の動作・状態・性質を表します。

主語(誰が)	一般動詞	その他の情報	意味
I	**work**	at the airport.	私は空港で働いています。
The bus	**leaves**	the station at 3:00.	そのバスは3時に駅を出発します。
Ken and I	**play**	basketball every day.	ケンと私は毎日バスケットボールをします。

▶主語がI / You以外の単数形で時制が現在の場合、一般動詞の語尾に-s [-es]をつけます。

● 否定文を作るときは、動詞の前に don't / doesn't をつけます。疑問文の場合は、主語の前に Do / Does を置きます。動詞はつねに原形です。

[肯定文] Lisa **likes** spicy food. リサは辛い食べ物が好きです。

[否定文] Lisa **doesn't like** spicy food. リサは辛い食べ物が好きではありません。

[疑問文] **Does** Lisa **like** spicy food? リサは辛い食べ物が好きですか。

● 命令文（「～しなさい」）は、主語を省略して動詞の原形から文を始めます。否定命令文（「～してはいけません」）は、文頭の動詞の前に Don't をつけます。

Open your textbook.
教科書を開きなさい。

Please close the window.
窓を閉めてください。

Don't take pictures here.
ここで写真を撮ってはいけません。

▶文頭の動詞の前にPleaseをつけると、「～してください」という丁寧な表現になります。

Hurry! The stores close soon.
Boutique

Grammar Checking

A (　　) 内から正しいほうの選択肢を選び、文を完成させましょう。　CheckLink

1. Bruce (**a.** has　**b.** have) three sisters.

2. Saki (**a.** study　**b.** studies) every night.

3. Do you and Maki (**a.** like　**b.** likes) horror movies?

4. Dave and I (**a.** play　**b.** plays) soccer on Sundays.

5. This coffee doesn't (**a.** taste　**b.** tastes) good.

6. (**a.** Are　**b.** Do) you usually eat breakfast?

7. James and his brother (**a.** don't　**b.** doesn't) live in the same city.

8. Please don't (**a.** bring　**b.** bringing) food into the classroom.

B 1と2の文を、それぞれ a) 否定文、b) Yes／Noをたずねる疑問文に書き換えましょう。

1. Emi and Ryo go to the same university.

a) ______________________________

b) ______________________________

2. Ryo takes a train downtown.

a) ______________________________

b) ______________________________

Reading ● *Travelog — San Francisco*

リョウの旅行日記を読み、紹介されている順に写真a～cに番号を振りましょう。

CheckLink DL 12 CD 12

Let's check out San Francisco. The Golden Gate Bridge is beautiful at night! It's 2,737 meters long. The cable cars are cool, and tickets don't cost much. Every year, 7 million people ride them! And don't forget Chinatown in downtown San Francisco. Fifteen thousand people live there. It has great restaurants and shops.

Note: cost「お金がかかる」

a. (　　)

b. (　　)

c. (　　)

Mission ! 2. あなた自身について書いてみよう！

(　　) に do / does / don't のいずれかを入れましょう。その後で、B のセリフの空所にあなた自身の情報を書き込んで、会話を完成させましょう。 DL 13 CD 13

A: I come to school by bus. How about you?

B: I come by ________________.

A: (　　　　　　) it take a long time?

B: It ____________ about ________ minutes. (　　　　　　) you have many classes today?

A: No, I (　　　　　　). I only have two classes. And you?

B: I ______________________________ today.

Unit 3 A British City in Canada?

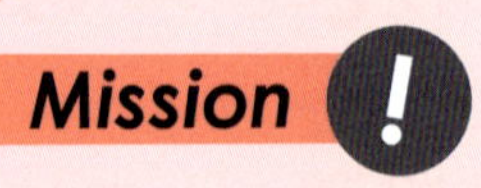

- 相手にお礼を言おう
- 代名詞を使った英文に慣れよう

Getting Ready

エミは、ビクトリア島に向かうフェリーに乗っています。

That's very kind of you.
a
b
c
d

A 1～4を表すイラストを上のa～dから選びましょう。

CheckLink　DL 14　CD 14

1. sunglasses (　　)　**2.** passenger (　　)　**3.** deck (　　)　**4.** island (　　)

B イラストを見ながら1～4の英文を聞きましょう。イラストと合っていればT、合っていなければFを選びましょう。

CheckLink　DL 15　CD 15

1. T / F　**2.** T / F　**3.** T / F　**4.** T / F

Conversation ● *On the Ferry to Victoria*

フェリーのデッキにて、エミは赤ちゃんを連れた夫婦と話しています。

A 会話を聞いて、聞き取った内容と合っているほうの選択肢を選びましょう。

CheckLink DL 16 CD 16

1. The baby is a (**a.** boy **b.** girl).
2. Diane and her husband live in (**a.** Toronto **b.** Victoria).
3. It's the couple's (**a.** first time **b.** second time) to visit Victoria.
4. It's (**a.** Diane's **b.** Danny's) idea to go to Butchart Gardens with Emi.

B もう一度会話を聞いて、空所を埋めましょう。

Emi: You're so cute!
Danny: Me?
Emi: No, your baby.
What's ([1]) name?
Danny: Oh! Ha ha ha! It's Amanda. I'm Danny, and this is my wife Diane.
Emi: Nice to meet ([2]).
I'm Emi. Do you live in Victoria?
Diane: No, we're from Toronto. This is ([3]) first time to visit Victoria.
Emi: It's ([4]), too. Do you know Butchart Gardens?
Diane: Yes, that's on our list of things to see. Right, Danny?
Danny: Yes, and ([5]) have a car. How about coming with ([6])?
Emi: **That's very kind of you.** Thank you!
Danny: You're very welcome.

Mission ! 1. セリフを言ってみよう！

音声を聞いて、下のセリフを確認しましょう。その後で、前のページのイラストを見ながら吹き出しのセリフを言ってみましょう。

DL 17 CD 17

That's very kind of you.

kind ofは、「カインダブ」のように音がつながります。音のつながりに注意しながら発音しましょう。

This is my friend Ryo. **He** is from Japan.
こちらは私の友人のリョウです。彼は日本から来ました。

● 代名詞は、「私（I）」「あなた・あなたたち（You）」のように話し手や相手を表します。また、前に出てきた名詞を言い換えるときに使います。

Mary and I saw a movie last night. **We** enjoyed **it** very much.
メアリーと私は昨夜映画を観ました。私たちはそれ（＝映画）をとても楽しみました。

● 代名詞は、文中での働きによって形を変えます。

主格 「～は/～が」 主語になる	所有格 「～の」 後ろに名詞が来る	目的格 「～を」 目的語になる 前置詞の後に来る	所有代名詞 「～のもの」
I	my	me	mine
you （単数・複数）	your	you	yours
he	his	him	his
she	her	her	hers
it	its	it	—
we	our	us	ours
they	their	them	theirs

● 所有格の代名詞は後ろに名詞を伴いますが、所有代名詞は単体で使います。

Your sneakers are cool.
— Thank you. **Yours** are cool, too.
あなたのスニーカー、かっこいいね。
— ありがとう。君のスニーカーもかっこいいよ。

Grammar Checking

A (　　) 内から正しいほうの選択肢を選び、文を完成させましょう。　CheckLink

1. Alice and (**a.** I　**b.** me) are roommates.

2. Roger plays (**a.** him　**b.** his) guitar every day.

3. Excuse me. Is this pen (**a.** your　**b.** yours)?

4. (**a.** She　**b.** Her) hobby is writing short stories.

5. That's not my textbook. It's (**a.** his　**b.** he's).

6. Here are your tickets. Please don't lose (**a.** it　**b.** them).

7. Our English teacher gives (**a.** our　**b.** us) a quiz every week.

8. Don't tell anyone (**a.** our　**b.** ours) secret.

B 下線部を適切な代名詞に変えて、文を書き換えましょう。

1. Diane and Danny have a baby.

____

2. The baby's name is Amanda.

____

3. The garden is very beautiful.

____

4. Please come with Danny and me.

____

5. This car is Diane's car and my car.

____

Reading　● *Travelog — Victoria*

エミの旅行日記を読み、紹介されている順に写真a〜cに番号を振りましょう。

 CheckLink　DL 18　 CD 18

In many ways, Victoria looks like a city in Great Britain. Its nickname is "the Garden City." My favorite garden there is Butchart Gardens. It's lovely. Also, there is afternoon tea at the Fairmont Empress Hotel. My tea was delicious, and very relaxing. Victoria even has a castle from the late 1800s — Craigdarroch Castle.

a. (　　)

b. (　　)

c. (　　)

Mission ! 2. あなた自身について書いてみよう！

Bのセリフの空所にあなた自身の情報を書き込んで、会話を完成させましょう。(　　)には代名詞を使いましょう。

DL 19　CD 19

A: **My** favorite class this year is American History. Professor Smith teaches **it**. **His** classes are always fun and lively. **He** doesn't give **us** much homework! Tell **me** about **your** favorite class this year.

B: OK. (　　　　) ______________ is ______________.

Professor ______________ teaches it. (　　　　) classes are ______________ and ______________. (　　　　) ______________.

Hints Spanish「スペイン語」　sociology「社会学」　literature「文学」　physical education「体育」　interesting「興味深い」　practical「実践的な」　easy to understand「分かりやすい」　assignment「宿題」　test「テスト」　report「レポート」

L.A. Style

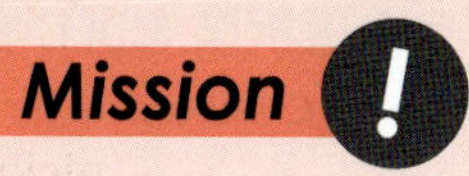

- 探しているものを伝えよう
- 進行形を使った英文に慣れよう

Getting Ready

ロサンゼルスに到着したリョウは、古着屋でショッピング中です。

I'm looking for a pair of vintage jeans.
a
b
c
d
Sale

A 1～4を表すイラストを上のa～dから選びましょう。

CheckLink DL 20 CD 20

1. customer ( )　　**3.** fitting room ( )

2. salesclerk ( )　　**4.** earrings ( )

B イラストを見ながら1～4の英文を聞きましょう。イラストと合っていればT、合っていなければFを選びましょう。

CheckLink DL 21 CD 21

1. T / F　**2.** T / F　**3.** T / F　**4.** T / F

Conversation ● *Shopping in L.A.*

リョウは古着屋の店員と話しています。

A 会話を聞いて、聞き取った内容と合っているほうの選択肢を選びましょう。

CheckLink DL 22 CD 22

1. Ryo is shopping for a pair of (**a.** denim **b.** leather) pants.
2. Ryo wants a (**a.** wide **b.** narrow) leg.
3. A (**a.** man **b.** woman) was in the fitting room.
4. The pants cost (**a.** $17 **b.** $70).

B もう一度会話を聞いて、空所を埋めましょう。

Ryo: Excuse me. **I'm looking for a pair of vintage jeans.**
Clerk: (1) you looking for a wide leg or a narrow leg?
Ryo: I'm (2) of getting a narrow leg.
Clerk: Do you like these? A lot of guys are (3) this style.
Ryo: Yeah, they're nice. (4) anyone using the fitting room?
Clerk: Yes, but... ah, she's (5) out now. Go ahead.
(a few minutes later)
Ryo: They feel nice, and the size is perfect. I'll take them.
Clerk: Excellent! That's $70, please.
Ryo: Seventeen dollars. That's so cheap!
Clerk: No... Umm... They're... Umm...
Ryo: I know. They're $70. I (6) just joking.

Mission ! 1. セリフを言ってみよう！

音声を聞いて、下のセリフを確認しましょう。その後で、前のページのイラストを見ながら吹き出しのセリフを言ってみましょう。

DL 23 CD 23

> ***I'm looking for a pair of vintage jeans.***

ジーンズは左右の足で1着になるため、(a pair of) jeansのように複数形で表します。

Breaking Down the Grammar　● 現在進行形・過去進行形

I **am playing** an online game now.

私は今、オンラインゲームをしています。

● 現在あるいは過去のある時点で進行中の動作を表す場合や、習慣的に行っていることを表す場合、進行形を使います。

主語	be動詞＋一般動詞の -ing形	その他の情報	意味
I	**am waiting**	for the bus.	私はバスを待っています。
Many people	**are using**	this app.	たくさんの人々がこのアプリを使っています。
I	**was doing**	my homework this morning.	私は今朝、宿題をやっていました。
Bob and Kai	**were** always **smiling**	at work.	ボブとカイはいつも職場で笑っていました。

▶習慣的に行っていることを表すとき、always「いつも」やoften「よく」などの副詞を使います。

● 否定文を作るときは、be動詞の後ろにnotをつけます。疑問文を作るときは、主語の前にbe動詞を置きます。

［肯定文］ They **are practicing** judo now. 彼らは今、柔道の練習をしています。

［否定文］ They **are not practicing** judo now. 彼らは今、柔道の練習をしていません。

［疑問文］ **Are** they **practicing** judo now? 彼らは今、柔道の練習をしていますか。

Grammar Checking

A (　　) 内から正しいほうの選択肢を選び、文を完成させましょう。 CheckLink

1. Ryo (**a.** writes　**b.** is writing) a postcard now.

2. Were (**a.** you studying　**b.** studying you) this morning?

3. (**a.** It　**b.** It's) not raining now.

4. Are you (**a.** a computer game playing　**b.** playing a computer game)?

5. Sorry, I (**a.** was　**b.** wasn't) listening.

6. Please wait a minute. I'm (**a.** drying my hair　**b.** my hair is drying).

7. Many people (**a.** are　**b.** is) waiting for a bus.

8. No one (**a.** was　**b.** wasn't) playing in the park.

B 太字になっている語句を (　　) 内で示されている形に合うように変えて、文を作りましょう。

1. Ryo / **shop** / in Los Angeles (現在進行形)

____

2. he / **look for** / a pair of vintage jeans (現在進行形の Yes-No 疑問文)

____

3. a customer / **use** / the fitting room (過去進行形)

____

4. she / **try on** / a dress (過去進行形の Yes-No 疑問文)

____

Reading ● *Travelog — L.A.'s Venice Beach*

リョウの旅行日記を読み、紹介されている順に写真a～cに番号を振りましょう。

CheckLink DL 24 CD 24

I was in Venice Beach today. It was crowded with people, but it was really cool! Some people were sitting at outdoor cafés and watching the people walk by. Others were lying on the beach and talking with friends. Some young guys were skateboarding. And me? I was shopping for vintage clothes.

a. (　　)

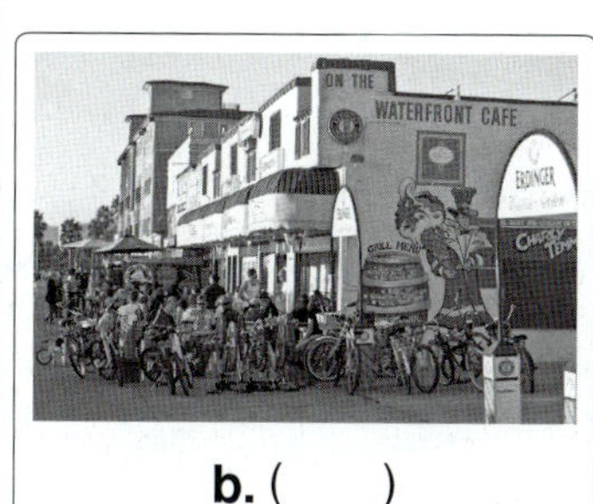

b. (　　)

c. (　　)

Mission ! 2. あなた自身について書いてみよう！

Bのセリフの空所にあなた自身の情報を書き込んで、会話を完成させましょう（進行形を使いましょう）。

DL 25 CD 25

A: I called you three times yesterday, but there was no answer. What were you doing at 7:00 a.m., 3:00 p.m. and 11:00 p.m.?

B: At 7:00 a.m., I was ______________________. At 3:00 p.m., I ____________ ______________, and at 11:00 p.m., ______________________.

A: Oh. And what are you doing now?

B: I ______________________________.

Hints study「勉強する」 do homework「宿題をする」 read a magazine「雑誌を読む」 watch TV「テレビを見る」 have lunch「お昼を食べる」 ride the train「電車に乗る」

Unit 5 The Canadian Rockies

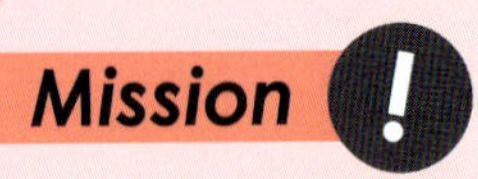

- 相手にお願いをしよう
- 時と場所を表す前置詞の使い方に慣れよう

Getting Ready

エミは、カナディアン・ロッキーで人生初の乗馬に挑戦することにしました。

Please wait for a minute.
a
b
c
d

A 1～4を表すイラストを上のa～dから選びましょう。

CheckLink　DL 26　CD 26

1. blanket (　　)　**2.** gloves (　　)　**3.** saddle (　　)　**4.** trail leader (　　)

B イラストを見ながら1～4の英文を聞きましょう。イラストと合っていればT、合っていなければFを選びましょう。

CheckLink　DL 27　CD 27

1. T / F　**2.** T / F　**3.** T / F　**4.** T / F

Conversation ● *Horseback Riding*

乗馬ツアーの開始前、エミとトレーナーが会話をしています。

A 会話を聞いて、聞き取った内容と合っているほうの選択肢を選びましょう。

CheckLink DL 28 CD 28

1. The trail leader's name is (**a.** Buck **b.** Sparky).
2. Emi's horse is very (**a.** gentle **b.** old).
3. Emi puts her (**a.** left **b.** right) hand on the saddle.
4. The ride starts at (**a.** 4:00 **b.** 5:00).

B もう一度会話を聞いて、空所を埋めましょう。

Buck: Hi. I'm Buck, your trail leader. And you're standing ([1]) ([2]) Sparky.

Emi: *(to Buck)* Hi, Sparky. My name's Emi.

Buck: Ha ha ha! No, I'm Buck. Your horse is Sparky.

Emi: Oh, sorry. I'm a little nervous ([3]) the ride.

Buck: Don't worry. Sparky is very gentle. Here, let me help you get on.

Emi: **Please wait for a minute.** ...*Whooo!* ...OK, I'm ready.

Buck: Put your left foot ([4]) this part, and your right hand ([5]) the saddle. Now pull yourself up onto the saddle. UP! Good job!

Emi: Yay!

Buck: We leave ([6]) 4:00.

Emi: OK, thanks.

Mission ! 1. セリフを言ってみよう！

音声を聞いて、下のセリフを確認しましょう。その後で、前のページのイラストを見ながら吹き出しのセリフを言ってみましょう。 DL 29 CD 29

> ***Please wait for a minute.***

「ちょっと待って」という表現には、他にもWait a minute. / Wait a second. / Just a moment.などがあります。

Breaking Down the Grammar ●時と場所を表す前置詞

My uncle lives **in** Los Angeles.
私のおじはロサンゼルスに住んでいます。

●時や場所を表す場合は、前置詞を使います。前置詞の後ろには名詞が続きます。

時を表す前置詞	例文
at [時刻]に **on** [日付や曜日]に	The bus arrives **at** noon **on** Sundays. そのバスは毎週日曜日の正午に到着します。
before [時刻・出来事など]より前に	Please be here **before** 7:00 tonight. 今夜7時より前にここにいてください。
for [期間]の間	Miranda stayed in Thailand **for** three weeks. ミランダはタイに3週間滞在しました。
in [月・季節・年・午前／午後など]に	School starts **in** September in the U.S. アメリカでは学校は9月に始まります。

場所を表す前置詞	例文
under ～の下方に・で **in** ～の中に・で	We took a walk **in** the park **under** the stars. 私たちは星空の下で公園の中を散歩しました。
on ～の上に・で	Peter put his jacket **on** the sofa. ピーターはジャケットをソファの上に置きました。
next to ～のそばに・で	I want to live **next to** the river someday. 私はいつの日か川沿いに住みたいです。

Grammar Checking

A (　　) 内から正しいほうの選択肢を選び、文を完成させましょう。 CheckLink

1. My first class starts (**a.** at **b.** for) 1:00 today.
2. Janet has a doctor's appointment (**a.** at **b.** on) Wednesday.
3. The cherry blossoms are lovely (**a.** in **b.** on) spring.
4. Maki studies English (**a.** for **b.** in) one hour every day.
5. There are many fish (**a.** in **b.** on) this lake.
6. Greg is standing (**a.** next to **b.** under) Brenda.
7. Don't forget your keys. They're (**a.** in **b.** on) the table.
8. The subway runs (**a.** in **b.** under) this street.

B 空所に適切な前置詞を入れましょう。1～8は**at** / **on** / **in**のいずれかを入れて時を表す表現に、9～16は**in** / **on** / **next to** / **under**のいずれかを入れてそれぞれのものの場所を表す表現にしましょう。

1. ________ Sunday
2. ________ my birthday
3. ________ midnight
4. ________ September
5. ________ spring
6. ________ 4:30
7. ________ 2020
8. ________ the afternoon
9. a whiteboard ➡ ____________ the classroom
10. a saucer ➡ ____________ a cup
11. Room 517 ➡ ____________ Room 516
12. a hat ➡ ____________ your head
13. water ➡ ____________ the bridge
14. a pilot ➡ ____________ a co-pilot
15. coffee ➡ ____________ the pot
16. a bath mat ➡ ____________ the floor

Reading　Travelog — Banff National Park

エミの旅行日記を読み、紹介されている順に写真a～cに番号を振りましょう。

DL 30　CD 30

I'm in Banff National Park. This morning, I was canoeing on beautiful Lake Louise. It was very peaceful. In the afternoon, I was riding in the Banff Gondola. It goes to the top of Sulphur Mountain in eight minutes. What a view! At night, I was relaxing at the Banff Upper Hot Springs. Ahhh!!!

a. (　　)

b. (　　)

c. (　　)

Mission ! 2. あなた自身について書いてみよう！

Aのセリフの空所にあなた自身の情報を書き込んで、会話を完成させましょう。

DL 31　CD 31

A: Do you have a busy schedule today?

B: Yes, I have three classes in the afternoon — from 1:00 to 6:00. I also have a dance lesson near my station tonight. How about you?

A: Well, I ______________________________

____

______________________________.

Hints club activity「クラブ活動」　part-time job「アルバイト」　doctor's appointment「医者の予約」　date「デート」　soccer practice「サッカーの練習」　piano lesson「ピアノのレッスン」

Unit 6 The Grand Canyon

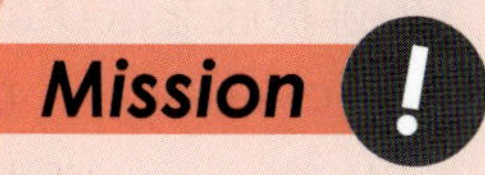

Mission !
- 単位の違いを理解しよう
- 可算名詞・不可算名詞の使い方に慣れよう

Getting Ready

グランドキャニオンに到着したリョウ。ハヴァス滝までトレッキングに挑戦です。

Is a gallon about one liter?
d
a
b
c

A 1～4を表すイラストを上のa～dから選びましょう。

CheckLink DL 32 CD 32

1. hiking first-aid kit ( )
2. hiking boots ( )
3. hiking poles ( )
4. hiking trail ( )

B イラストを見ながら1～4の英文を聞きましょう。イラストと合っていればT、合っていなければFを選びましょう。

CheckLink DL 33 CD 33

1. T / F **2.** T / F **3.** T / F **4.** T / F

Conversation ● *Taking a Hike*

出発前、リョウは近くにいた女性に話しかけてみました。

A 会話を聞いて、聞き取った内容と合っているほうの選択肢を選びましょう。

CheckLink DL 34 CD 34

1. It's about (**a.** 10 **b.** 16) kilometers to Havasupai Falls.
2. It takes about (**a.** three **b.** five) hours to hike to the falls.
3. A gallon is about (**a.** two **b.** four) liters.
4. Anna put some sunscreen on Ryo's (**a.** face **b.** neck).

B もう一度会話を聞いて、空所を埋めましょう。

Ryo: Good morning. Are you hiking to Havasupai Falls?
Anna: That's right. It's 10 ([1]), about 16 kilometers.
Ryo: So, it takes about three ([2])?
Anna: Yes. I hope you have lots of ([3]). You need about a gallon.
Ryo: **Is a gallon about one liter?**
Anna: No, it's this much. *(holding out two big bottles of water)*
Ryo: Oh, that's about four ([4]).
...Yeah, I'm OK.
Anna: Good. Hey, how about hiking to the ([5]) together?
Ryo: Perfect! I mean, yes. Thank you. By the way, I'm Ryo.
Anna: I'm Anna. Here, let me put some ([6]) on your face.

Mission ! 1. セリフを言ってみよう！

音声を聞いて、下のセリフを確認しましょう。その後で、前のページのイラストを見ながら吹き出しのセリフを言ってみましょう。 DL 35 CD 35

"*Is a gallon about one liter?*"

アメリカのスーパーでは、ジュースや牛乳、アイスクリームも1ガロン（約4リットル）の単位で売られています。

Breaking Down the Grammar ● 可算名詞・不可算名詞

基本
例文

I have two bananas and a cup of tea for breakfast.
私は朝食にバナナ２本と紅茶１杯をとります。

● 英語の名詞には、数えられるもの（可算名詞）と数えられないもの（不可算名詞）があります。可算名詞にはa / anがつき、複数形は以下のように作ります。

語尾にsをつける	cat – cats / room – rooms / apple – apples
語尾にesをつける （s, o, sh, ch, x で終わる単語）	class – classes / tomato – tomatoes / wish – wishes / peach – peaches / box – boxes
語尾を変えて-s/-esをつける （子音＋ y、f/fe で終わる単語）	party – parties / country – countries / leaf – leaves / knife – knives
不規則変化する	tooth – teeth / man – men / mouse – mice / child – children

● 不可算名詞にはa / anはつかず、数量や単位を表す語句を使って数量を表します。

種類	例	数量を表す表現
物質名詞	wood（木材）、salt（塩）、 toast（トースト）、meat（肉）、water（水）、 ice cream（アイスクリーム）	a teaspoon of salt 小さじ１杯の塩 a slice of meat 一切れの肉 a glass of water グラス１杯の水
抽象名詞	time（時間）、love（愛情）、anger（怒り）、 information（情報）	some time いくらかの時間 a lot of love たくさんの愛情
集合名詞	police（警察）、furniture（家具類）、 hair（毛髪）、baggage（手荷物）、	a piece of furniture １つの家具 a piece of baggage １つの手荷物

▶集合名詞の多くは数えられる名詞として扱われることが多く、通常は複数形扱いですが、-s/-esはつきません。

例：Many **people** are waiting for the bus.
たくさんの人々がバスを待っています。

Two glasses of milk, please.

Grammar Checking

A (　　) 内から正しいほうの選択肢を選び、文を完成させましょう。 CheckLink

1. Do you have a lot of (**a.** class **b.** classes) today?

2. My favorite dessert is (**a.** ice cream **b.** an ice cream).

3. Bring (**a.** a **b.** an) umbrella today.

4. She doesn't eat (**a.** meat **b.** a meat).

5. Do you want (**a.** cup of a coffee **b.** a cup of coffee)?

6. Steve has (**a.** big blue eyes **b.** big blue eye).

7. I love your (**a.** hair **b.** hairs)!

8. Kensuke never has (**a.** a time **b.** time) to eat lunch.

B 例にならって、次の文が正しければ○、間違っていれば×をつけた上で正しい文に直しましょう。

[×] **1.** The ~~person~~ *people* in this picture are Bill and Janet.

[　] **2.** Emi loves strawberry.

[　] **3.** Ryo likes all kinds of music.

[　] **4.** That's a nice shirts. Is it new?

[　] **5.** Please help me with my homework.

[　] **6.** Do you always brush your tooth after dinner?

[　] **7.** I love your new shoes.

[　] **8.** Jane always eats two piece of toasts for breakfast.

Reading　● *Travelog — Canyon Pics*

リョウの旅行日記を読み、紹介されている順に写真a～cに番号を振りましょう。

CheckLink　DL 36　CD 36

The Grand Canyon is in Arizona, and it's BIG! It's 446 km long, 29 km wide and 1,800 m deep in some places. The Colorado River runs through the Grand Canyon for about 450 km. My hike to Havasupai Falls was great, and the waterfall was beautiful. Camping there was a lot of fun, too.

a. (　　)

b. (　　)

c. (　　)

Mission ! 2. あなた自身について書いてみよう！

あなたは友人とハワイ旅行に行くことになり、その準備について話しています。会話中の（　　）にa / an / someのいずれかを書き入れ、その後で、Bのセリフの空所を自由に埋めて、会話を完成させましょう。

DL 37　CD 37

A: Let's go shopping before our trip to Hawaii. I have (　　　　) list of things to buy.

B: Oh, OK. What's on your list?

A: Well, I need (　　　　) guidebook, (　　　　) sunscreen and (　　　　) electronic dictionary［電子辞書］. What do you need?

B: I need to get ______________________________, ______________________________ and ______________________________.

Hints swimsuit「水着」 sunglasses「サングラス」 sandals「サンダル」 sun hat「日よけの帽子」 suitcase「スーツケース」 backpack「リュックサック」 shampoo「シャンプー」

T.O. — Toronto, Ontario

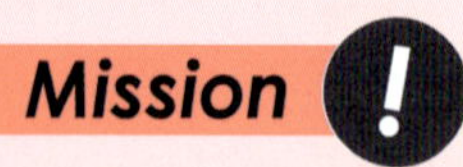

- 感想を述べよう
- 一般動詞の過去形を使った英文に慣れよう

Getting Ready

エミは、トロントでタクシーに乗りました。

Yes, I enjoyed every minute!
TAXI
a
b
c
d

A 1～4を表すイラストを上のa～dから選びましょう。

CheckLink DL 38 CD 38

1. back seat ( )　　**3.** seat belt ( )

2. headrest ( )　　**4.** steering wheel ( )

B イラストを見ながら1～4の英文を聞きましょう。イラストと合っていればT、合っていなければFを選びましょう。

CheckLink DL 39 CD 39

1. T / F　　**2.** T / F　　**3.** T / F　　**4.** T / F

Conversation

Emi's Taxi Ride

バスターミナルへと向かうタクシーの中で、運転手とエミが話しています。

A 会話を聞いて、聞き取った内容と合っているほうの選択肢を選びましょう。

CheckLink　DL 40　CD 40

1. The taxi driver says that Toronto is a (**a.** big **b.** great) city.
2. People from all over the world (**a.** live in **b.** visit) Toronto.
3. Emi didn't try (**a.** Brazilian **b.** Indian) food.
4. The driver is from (**a.** Africa **b.** Jamaica).

B もう一度会話を聞いて、空所を埋めましょう。

Driver: Did you ([1]) a nice time in Toronto?

Emi: **Yes, I enjoyed every minute!** I ([2]) have time to see it all.

Driver: It's a great city. People from all over the world live here.

Emi: Yes, I ([3]) people from many different countries.

Driver: The food here is very good, too.

Emi: It's amazing! I ([4]) all kinds — Indian curry, Jamaican carrot juice, African lamb wraps…

Driver: I'm from Africa. ([5]) you like the lamb wraps?

Emi: I ([6]) them!

Driver: I'm happy to hear that. …Well, here we are at the bus terminal.

Note: lamb wraps「仔羊肉のラップサンド」

Mission! 1. セリフを言ってみよう！

音声を聞いて、下のセリフを確認しましょう。その後で、前のページのイラストを見ながら吹き出しのセリフを言ってみましょう。　DL 41　CD 41

Yes, I enjoyed every minute!

every minuteは、ここでは「一瞬一瞬、全ての瞬間」という意味で、enjoy every minuteで「満喫する」という意味になります。

Breaking Down the Grammar ● 一般動詞の過去形

We visited the flea market last weekend.
私たちは先週末、フリーマーケットを訪れました。

● 過去の動作や状態を表すときは、一般動詞の過去形を使います。

主語	一般動詞	その他の情報	意味
We	**played**	online games together.	私たちは一緒にオンラインゲームをしました。
The driver	**took**	me to the station.	その運転手は私を駅まで連れて行ってくれました。

● 一般動詞の過去形には、規則変化するものと不規則変化するものがあります。

規則変化する動詞（語尾に -ed をつける）	ask – ask**ed** / play – play**ed** / watch – watch**ed** / like – like**d** / try – tr**ied** / stop – stop**ped**
不規則変化する動詞	have – **had** / eat – **ate** / go – **went** / have – **had** / take – **took** / catch – **caught** / know – **knew** / read – **read** / run – **ran** / meet – **met** / see – **saw**

▶不規則変化する動詞は、巻末の「不規則変化動詞一覧」でもチェックしましょう。

● 否定文を作るときは、動詞の前に didn't をつけます。疑問文を作るときは、主語の前に Did を置きます。どちらも動詞は原形です。

［肯定文］Bob and Sally **bought** a new car.
ボブとサリーは新しい車を買いました。

［否定文］They **didn't buy** a new car.
彼らは新しい車を買いませんでした。

［疑問文］**Did** they **buy** a new car?
彼らは新しい車を買いましたか。

Did your dog eat your homework again, Tommy?

Grammar Checking

A (　　) 内から正しいほうの選択肢を選び、文を完成させましょう。 CheckLink

1. Adam and his friends (**a.** played **b.** were played) basketball on Sunday.

2. Did you (**a.** go **b.** went) shopping yesterday?

3. Mary was very busy today. She (**a.** not had **b.** didn't have) time for lunch.

4. Julia is sick. She (**a.** did caught **b.** caught) a cold.

5. I (**a.** ran **b.** run) to the train station this morning.

6. (**a.** Did you **b.** Did you do) your homework?

7. We didn't (**a.** knew **b.** know) anyone at the party.

8. (**a.** Did you stay **b.** Were you stayed) at a nice hotel?

B 空所に入る動詞を枠内から選び、過去形にして書き入れましょう。その後、あなた自身が今日したことにチェック [✓] をつけましょう。

clean (掃除する)	do (する)	eat (食べる)	go (行く)
meet (会う)	read (読む)	take (とる)	watch (見る)

Last night...

[　　] **1.** I ______________ homework.

[　　] **2.** I ______________ a shower.

[　　] **3.** I ______________ dinner after 7:00.

[　　] **4.** I ______________ TV.

[　　] **5.** I ______________ a friend.

[　　] **6.** I ______________ to bed before 12:00.

[　　] **7.** I ______________ my room.

[　　] **8.** I ______________ a book.

Reading ● *Travelog — Kensington Market*

エミの旅行日記を読み、紹介されている順に写真a～cに番号を振りましょう。

CheckLink DL 42 CD 42

I visited Kensington Market, a multicultural neighborhood in downtown Toronto. It had everything — food from everywhere in the world, vintage clothes, unique restaurants and cafés, and much more. I walked by Victorian houses, saw some wonderful graffiti and listened to street artists. This area became a World Heritage Site in 2006.

Notes: multicultural neighborhood「多文化的な地域」 World Heritage Site「世界遺産」

a. (　　)

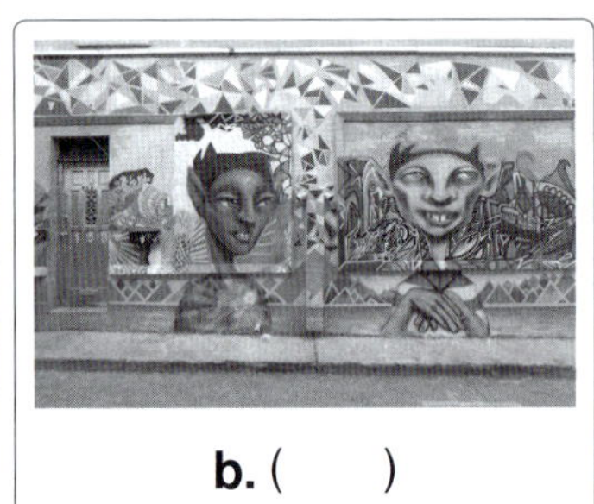
b. (　　)

c. (　　)

Mission ! 2. あなた自身について書いてみよう！

Aのセリフの空所にあなた自身の情報を書き込んで、会話を完成させましょう（過去形を使いましょう）。

DL 43 CD 43

A: What did you do on Sunday?

B: Well, I cleaned my room in the morning. In the afternoon, I went shopping. And at night, I watched a movie on DVD. What did you do?

A: In the morning, I ____________________. I ____________________ in the afternoon. And at night, ____________________.

Hints get a haircut「髪を切る」 play the guitar「ギターを弾く」 meet a friend「友達に会う」

Big Texas

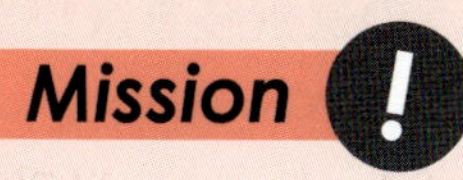

● 会話を続けよう
● 疑問詞の使い方に慣れよう

Getting Ready

リョウは、テキサスのヒューストンでロデオを観戦中です。

A 1～4を表すイラストを上のa～dから選びましょう。

CheckLink DL 44 CD 44

1. bull (　　) **2.** bull rider (　　) **3.** clown (　　) **4.** clown barrel (　　)

B イラストを見ながら1～4の英文を聞きましょう。それぞれ、質問とそれに対する答えが流れます。イラストと合っていればT、合っていなければFを選びましょう。

CheckLink DL 45 CD 45

1. T / F **2.** T / F **3.** T / F **4.** T / F

Conversation　● *A Texas Rodeo*

リョウは、隣に座っていた女性とロデオについて話しています。

A 会話を聞いて、聞き取った内容と合っているほうの選択肢を選びましょう。

CheckLink　DL 46　CD 46

1. The lady went to her first rodeo (**a.** at the age of 4　**b.** 4 years ago).

2. Ryo says the bull riding looks (**a.** dangerous　**b.** fun).

3. A bull weighs about (**a.** 500　**b.** 1,500) pounds.

4. Hank is a (**a.** bull rider　**b.** clown).

B もう一度会話を聞いて、空所を埋めましょう。

Lady: Hi. ([1]　　　　　　　　) are you from?
Ryo: I'm from Japan. **How about you?**
Lady: I'm from Texas. Is this your first rodeo?
Ryo: Yes, it is. It's really exciting!
Lady: Yeah, I love rodeos.
Ryo: ([2]　　　　　　　　) did you ([3]　　　　　　　　) to your first rodeo?
Lady: I was four years old. I love the bull riding.
Ryo: It looks dangerous. ([4]　　　　　　　　) ([5]　　　　　　　　) does a bull ([6]　　　　　　　　)?
Lady: About 1,500 pounds. ...Oh, there's my husband. Go Hank!
Ryo: Your husband is a great bull rider. He's so cool!
Lady: Oh, that's not my husband. My husband is the clown.

Note: pound「ポンド（重さの単位。1ポンドは約450グラム）」

Mission ! 1. セリフを言ってみよう！

音声を聞いて、下のセリフを確認しましょう。その後で、前のページのイラストを見ながら吹き出しのセリフを言ってみましょう。　DL 47　CD 47

How about you?

 How about you?は「あなたはどうですか」という意味で、相手から聞かれたことと同じ内容を相手にたずねるときに使える便利な表現です。

Breaking Down the Grammar ● 疑問詞

Where do you live?
あなたはどこに住んでいますか。

●「誰／何／いつ／どこ」などの情報をたずねる疑問文では、疑問詞を使います。
疑問詞は文頭に置かれ、be動詞やdo / does / didを使った疑問文が続きます。

疑問詞	例文
who 「誰」	**Who** is the girl in this picture? この写真に写っている少女は誰ですか。 **Who** made these cookies? 誰がこのクッキーを作りましたか。 ▶「誰が～しますか」とたずねるときは、Whoの直後に動詞が来ます。
what 「何」	**What** is your favorite food? あなたの好きな食べ物は何ですか。 **What** sports do you play? あなたは何のスポーツをプレーしますか。 **What** kind of music does Jessica like? ジェシカは何の音楽が好きですか。
when 「いつ」	**When** is your birthday? あなたの誕生日はいつですか。 **When** did you eat lunch? あなたはいつ昼食を食べましたか。
where 「どこ」	**Where** is the new bookstore? その新しい本屋はどこにありますか。 **Where** does Jack live? ジャックはどこに住んでいますか。
why 「なぜ」	**Why** were you late? あなたはなぜ遅刻したのですか。
how 「どのように・どのくらい」	**How** much is this bag? このカバンはいくらですか。 **How** long is your summer vacation? あなたの夏休みはどのくらい長いですか。

Grammar Checking

A (　　) 内から正しいほうの選択肢を選び、文を完成させましょう。 CheckLink

1. (**a.** What **b.** Who) is your name?

2. (**a.** When **b.** Where) is George's birthday?

3. (**a.** What **b.** Why) did you do that?

4. (**a.** Where **b.** What) does Mari live?

5. How (**a.** long **b.** time) does it take you to get to school?

6. (**a.** When **b.** Who) broke the window?

7. How (**a.** big **b.** size) is your apartment?

8. What (**a.** do you like color **b.** color do you like)?

B (　　) 内の語句を並べ替えて、日本語に合う文を作りましょう。

1. (party / when / the / does / start) パーティーはいつ始まりますか。

______________________________?

2. (friend / who / your / is / best) あなたの一番の友達は誰ですか。

______________________________?

3. (you / did / lunch / where / have) あなたはどこでお昼を食べましたか。

______________________________?

4. (much / these / how / are / boots) このブーツはいくらですか。

______________________________?

5. (is / favorite / your / subject / what) あなたの好きな科目は何ですか。

______________________________?

Reading ● *Travelog — Dinner Texas Style*

リョウの旅行日記を読み、紹介されている順に写真a～cに番号を振りましょう。

CheckLink DL 48 

Today I had dinner at a restaurant in Amarillo, Texas. For a starter, I had a salad. What was the main dish? That's right — a big juicy sirloin steak. How big was it? It was 21 ounces, or about 600 grams. I was full, but I ordered a brownie for dessert. Why did I order dessert? Just look at the photo. Mmm!

a. (　　)

b. (　　)

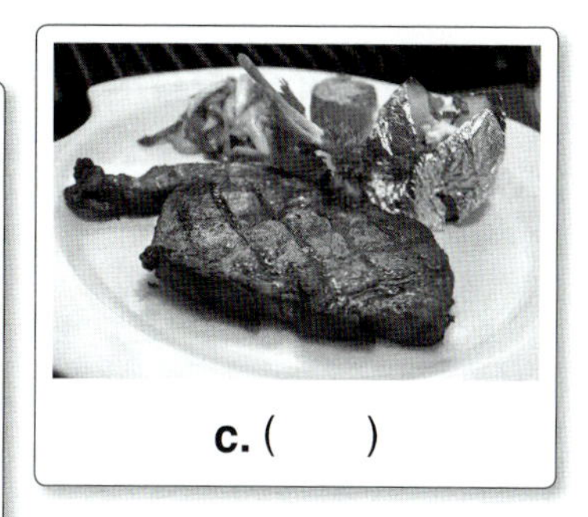

c. (　　)

Mission ! 2. あなた自身について書いてみよう！

(　　) に正しい疑問詞を入れましょう。その後で、Bのセリフの空所にあなた自身の情報を書き込んで、会話を完成させましょう。

DL 49 CD 49

A: (　　　　　　) is the name of your favorite restaurant? [好きなレストランの名前は何ですか]

B: My favorite restaurant is ________________________________.

A: (　　　　　　) do you like it? [なぜそのレストランが好きなのですか]

B: I like it because ________________________________.

A: (　　　　　　) was the last time you went there? [最後にそこへ行ったのはいつですか]

B: I ________________________________.

Hints fresh「新鮮な」 healthy「健康的な」 delicious「おいしい」 inexpensive「値段が手頃」 have a nice atmosphere「雰囲気がよい」 quiet「静かな」 ~days / weeks / months ago「～日／週／月前に」

Unit 9

Ottawa — The Capital

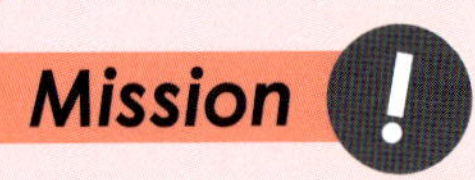

- 食べ物を注文しよう
- 接続詞を使った英文に慣れよう

Getting Ready

エミは、オタワ生まれのちょっと変わった食べ物を発見したようです。

A 1～4を表すイラストを上のa～dから選びましょう。

CheckLink　DL 50　CD 50

1. cashier (　　)　**2.** menu board (　　)　**3.** stand (　　)　**4.** sundae (　　)

B イラストを見ながら1～4の英文を聞きましょう。イラストと合っていればT、合っていなければFを選びましょう。

CheckLink　DL 51　CD 51

1. T / F　**2.** T / F　**3.** T / F　**4.** T / F

Conversation ● *One BeaverTail, Please*

エミは店員にメニューについてたずねています。

A 会話を聞いて、聞き取った内容と合っているほうの選択肢を選びましょう。

CheckLink DL 52 CD 52

1. A BeaverTail is (**a.** a Canadian hamburger **b.** like a donut).
2. A BeaverTail is (**a.** sweet **b.** spicy).
3. Emi orders a (**a.** Maple Butter **b.** Banana Chocolate) BeaverTail.
4. Emi orders a small (**a.** hot coffee **b.** iced tea) with her BeaverTail.

B もう一度会話を聞いて、空所を埋めましょう。

Cashier: Did you come for a BeaverTail ([1]) a drink?

Emi: A beaver tail? Is that a Canadian hamburger?

Cashier: Ha ha ha! No, it's like a donut, ([2]) there's no hole in it. It looks like a beaver's tail, ([3]) it's soft and sweet.

Emi: Oh, they look delicious! I think I want Cinnamon ([4]) Sugar...

Cashier: Good choice.

Emi: ... ([5]) Maple Butter.

Cashier: One Maple Butter?

Emi: Yes, please. Wait! No! **I like fruit, so I want Banana Chocolate.** And it's hot today, ([6]) I'd also like a small iced tea.

Mission ! 1. セリフを言ってみよう！

音声を聞いて、下のセリフを確認しましょう。その後で、前のページのイラストを見ながら吹き出しのセリフを言ってみましょう。 DL 53 CD 53

I like fruit, so I want Banana Chocolate.

soの発音は [sóu]で､｢ソー｣ のように伸ばすのではなく､｢ソゥ｣ となります。

Breaking Down the Grammar ● 接続詞 and / or / but / so

I have a piano, **but** I don't play it.
私はピアノを持っていますが、それを演奏しません。

● 接続詞は、２つ以上の語句や文をつなげる働きをします。

接続詞		例文
and 「AとB」 「AそしてB」	語句	My new smartphone is thin **and** light. 私の新しいスマートフォンは薄くて軽いです。
	文	Dan left home **and** went to the station. ダンは家を出て、そして駅に向かいました。
or 「AまたはB」 「AあるいはB」	語句	Would you like tea **or** coffee? 紅茶とコーヒー、どちらがいいですか。
	文	Did Ted call you, **or** did he text you? テッドはあなたに電話しましたか、それとも携帯メールを送りましたか。
but 「AだけれどB」 「AしかしB」	語句	The Japanese chess player is young **but** strong. その将棋棋士は若いけれど強いです。
	文	I love cats, **but** I have a cat allergy. 私は猫が大好きですが、猫アレルギーです。
so 「AなのでB」	文	Meg was hungry, **so** she ate three hamburgers. メグはお腹がすいていたので、ハンバーガーを３つ食べました。 We are late, **so** let's take a taxi. 私たちは遅れているので、タクシーに乗りましょう。

Grammar Checking

A (　　) 内から正しいほうの選択肢を選び、文を完成させましょう。 CheckLink

1. It's hot (**a.** and **b.** so) sunny today.
2. It's cool outside, (**a.** but **b.** so) bring a jacket.
3. Do you usually go to bed early (**a.** and **b.** or) late?
4. The restaurant is expensive, (**a.** but **b.** so) the food isn't very good.
5. We watched a movie (**a.** and **b.** so) played video games last night.
6. Diane's tooth hurt, (**a.** so **b.** but) she went to see a dentist.
7. Is Emily in her room, (**a.** but **b.** or) did she go out?
8. My train was late, (**a.** so **b.** but) I wasn't late for class.

B 例にならって、枠内にある語句を下線部に、and / or / but / so を [　] に書き入れて文を完成させましょう。

he never plays it	windy today	~~fall~~	he went to bed early
his brother is, too	was he lying	he opened the window	

1. Which do you like better, spring [or] fall ?
2. It's cold [　　] ____________________ .
3. He was very hot, [　　] ____________________ .
4. Sam has a guitar, [　　] ____________________ .
5. Was he telling the truth, [　　] ____________________ ?
6. Harry felt tired, [　　] ____________________ .
7. Ken is a doctor, [　　] ____________________ .

Reading　Travelog — On and Around the Hill

エミの旅行日記を読み、紹介されている順に写真a～cに番号を振りましょう。

CheckLink　DL 54　CD 54

Ottawa isn't a big city like Toronto, but it's lovely! I visited the Parliament Buildings today. The buildings are on a hill, so people call the area Parliament Hill, or simply the Hill. In the morning, I watched the Changing of the Guard ceremony. In the afternoon I walked along the beautiful Rideau Canal.

Notes: Parliament「国会」　Changing of the Guard「衛兵交代」　canal「運河」

a. (　　)

b. (　　)

c. (　　)

Mission ! 2. あなた自身について書いてみよう！

(　　)に and / but / or のいずれかを入れましょう。その後で、Bのセリフの空所にあなた自身の情報を書き込んで、会話を完成させましょう。　DL 55　CD 55

A: Last night, I stayed home (　　　　　　) studied. What did you do?

B: I ______________________ and ______________________.

A: Did you go to bed before midnight (　　　　　　) after midnight?

B: I ______________________ midnight.

A: I only slept for 4 hours, (　　　　　　) I'm not tired now. Are you sleepy?

B: ______________________, so ______________________.

Unit 10

Funky New Orleans

Mission !

- やりたいことを伝えよう
- 動名詞・不定詞を使った英文に慣れよう

Getting Ready

リョウは、ニューオリンズの街を巡るツアーに参加することにしました。

A 1～4を表すイラストを上のa～dから選びましょう。

CheckLink　DL 56　CD 56

1. pins (　　)　**2.** statue (　　)　**3.** tour conductor (　　)　**4.** tourist (　　)

B イラストを見ながら1～4の英文を聞きましょう。イラストと合っていればT、合っていなければFを選びましょう。

CheckLink　DL 57　CD 57

1. T / F　**2.** T / F　**3.** T / F　**4.** T / F

Conversation ● *I Hope You Like the Tour*

リョウは、ツアー参加者の名簿を持った添乗員の女性に話しかけています。

A 会話を聞いて、聞き取った内容と合っているほうの選択肢を選びましょう。

CheckLink DL 58 CD 58

1. Ryo's family name is (**a.** Hashimoto **b.** Matsumoto).
2. Ryo (**a.** knew **b.** didn't know) that New Orleans was famous for jazz.
3. Ryo plays the (**a.** bass **b.** piano).
4. The tour conductor tells Ryo to (**a.** take bass lessons **b.** continue to practice).

B もう一度会話を聞いて、空所を埋めましょう。

Tour Conductor (TC): Hi. I ([1]) to have your name, please.

Ryo: It's Ryo Hashimoto.

TC: Mr. Hashimoto. ...Ah, yes. Here you are. Do you ([2]) listening to jazz?

Ryo: Yes, it's my favorite kind of music. I ([3]) going to jazz clubs.

TC: Then you came to the right place. New Orleans is famous for jazz.

Ryo: That's why I ([4]) to come here. **I hope to meet some musicians.** I ([5]) to be a professional bass player. I'm not very good, though.

TC: Well, ([6]) practicing! I hope you like the tour.

Mission ! 1. セリフを言ってみよう！

音声を聞いて、下のセリフを確認しましょう。その後で、前のページのイラストを見ながら吹き出しのセリフを言ってみましょう。 DL 59 CD 59

> ***I hope to meet some musicians.***

musiciansは「ミュージシャン」のように,「ジ (si)」の部分を強く言います。日本語とはアクセントが違うので注意しましょう。

Breaking Down the Grammar　● 動名詞・不定詞

Jim **kept dancing** all night long.
ジムは一晩中踊り続けました。

●「ギターを弾くことを楽しむ」のように、1つの文中で2つ以上の動詞を使う場合、動名詞（~ing）や不定詞（to＋動詞の原形）を使います。

●後ろに動名詞が来る動詞：**enjoy, dislike, finish, keep, mind, avoid** など

主語＋一般動詞	動名詞	その他の情報	意味
We enjoyed	**camping**	in the mountains.	私たちは山でキャンプすることを楽しみました。

▶「現在あるいはこれまでに起こったことに対して何かする」という動詞が多い

●後ろに不定詞が来る動詞：**want, hope, need, decide, pretend, promise** など

主語＋一般動詞	不定詞	その他の情報	意味
Peter wants	**to visit**	Kyoto.	ピーターは京都を訪れたいです。

▶「あることをしようとする意欲や意図を表す」動詞が多い

●どちらでもよい動詞：**start, begin, love, like, continue** など

主語＋一般動詞	動名詞／不定詞	その他の情報	意味
I like	**looking** / **to look**	at stars.	私は星を見ることが好きです。

Grammar Checking

A (　　) 内から正しいほうの選択肢を選び、文を完成させましょう。　CheckLink

1. Ryo enjoys (**a.** meeting　**b.** to meet) new people.

2. Saki wants (**a.** living　**b.** to live) in Hawaii.

3. Jane started (**a.** taking のみ　**b.** taking または to take) dance lessons.

4. Did you finish (**a.** cleaning のみ　**b.** cleaning または to clean) your room?

5. I need (**a.** writing　**b.** to write) my report tonight.

6. Kendra loves (**a.** to draw のみ　**b.** drawing または to draw) pictures.

7. I hope (**a.** to travel　**b.** traveling) around the world someday.

8. Bob really dislikes (**a.** to wash　**b.** washing) clothes.

B 空所に入る動詞を枠内から選び、to不定詞または動名詞にして書き入れましょう。どちらでもよいときは両方書きましょう。

arrive (到着する)	buy (買う)	do (する)	play (プレーする)
ride (乗る)	swim (泳ぐ)	work (働く)	

1. Mark often goes to the beach. He enjoys ________________.

2. Maki is studying art history. She wants ________________ in a museum.

3. The boys finished ________________ soccer about an hour ago.

4. I need ________________ some things at the drugstore.

5. Haruki really dislikes ________________ crowded trains in the morning.

6. We hope ________________ in Kyoto before noon.

7. Jennifer likes ________________ her homework in a coffee shop.

Reading　Travelog — In the Deep South

リョウの旅行日記を読み、紹介されている順に写真a～cに番号を振りましょう。

 CheckLink　DL 60　 CD 60

People like to visit the French Quarter area of New Orleans for its music and food. I enjoyed listening to jazz. I dislike eating spicy food, but I wanted to try gumbo, a kind of stew. It was good, but HOT!!! I needed to drink LOTS of water. I also enjoyed cruising down the Mississippi River on a steamboat.

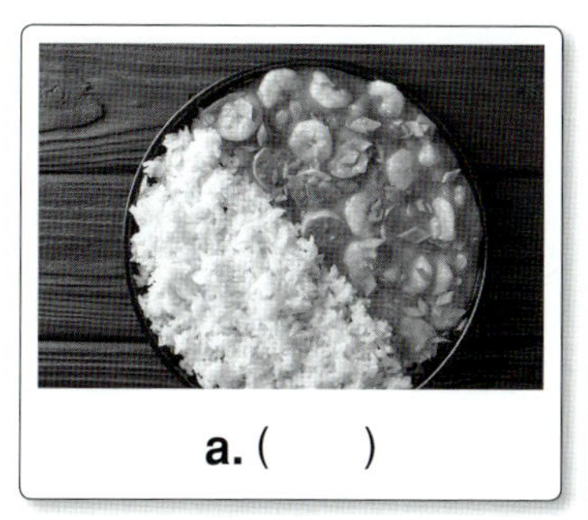

a. (　　)

b. (　　)

c. (　　)

Mission ! 2. あなた自身について書いてみよう！

Bのセリフの空所にあなた自身の情報を書き込んで、会話を完成させましょう（動名詞と不定詞を使いましょう）。

DL 61　CD 61

A: What do you like to do?

B: Well, I love ______________________________! I also enjoy ______________________________.

A: What do you dislike doing?

B: I dislike ______________________________. Oh, and I hate ______________________________!

Hints dance「踊る」　sing「歌う」　play sports「スポーツをする」　go to movies「映画に行く」　do laundry「洗たくをする」　get up early「早起きする」　cook「料理する」

Charming Quebec City

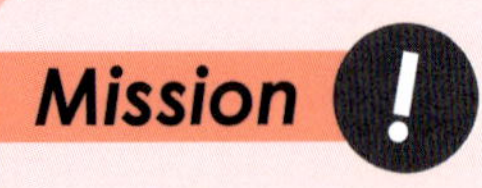

- 滞在日数を伝えよう
- 未来形を使った英文に慣れよう

Getting Ready

ケベックにいるエミは、似顔絵を描いてもらうことにしたようです。

A 1～4を表すイラストを上のa～dから選びましょう。

CheckLink　DL 62　CD 62

1. artist (　　)　**2.** caricature (　　)　**3.** drawing board (　　)　**4.** stool (　　)

B イラストを見ながら1～4の英文を聞きましょう。イラストと合っていればT、合っていなければFを選びましょう。

CheckLink　DL 63　CD 63

1. T / F　**2.** T / F　**3.** T / F　**4.** T / F

Conversation ● *Things to See and Do*

似顔絵を描いてもらう間、エミは絵描きとの会話を楽しんでいます。

A 会話を聞いて、聞き取った内容と合っているほうの選択肢を選びましょう。

CheckLink DL 64 CD 64

1. Emi will (**a.** draw lots of pictures **b.** take many photographs) of Old Quebec.
2. She will visit art museums (**a.** before **b.** after) walking around the city.
3. She (**a.** tried **b.** will have) meat pie and pea soup.
4. She (**a.** thinks **b.** doesn't think) she will like her caricature.

B もう一度会話を聞いて、空所を埋めましょう。

Artist: How long are you going to stay in Quebec City?

Emi: **I'll stay for two or three days.** It's so interesting!

Artist: What (1   ) you going to do?

Emi: First, (2   ) going to walk around Old Quebec and take lots of pictures. Then I think I'll (3   ) some art museums.

Artist: (4   ) love the art museums. They're excellent!

Emi: I'm also (5   ) to try some Quebec cuisine. My guidebook recommends meat pie and pea soup.

Artist: Good! ...OK, I finished your caricature. I hope you like it.

Emi: I'm sure I (6   ). ...Ha ha ha! I love it! Thank you.

Notes: cuisine「料理」 meat pie「ミートパイ」 pea soup「豆のスープ」

Mission ! 1. セリフを言ってみよう！

音声を聞いて、下のセリフを確認しましょう。その後で、前のページのイラストを見ながら吹き出しのセリフを言ってみましょう。 DL 65 CD 65

I'll stay for two or three days.

会話ではI willをI'll（発音：アイル）、She willをShe'll（発音：シール）のように短くして言うことが多いです。

Breaking Down the Grammar ● 未来形

I **am going to** study economics in college.
私は大学で経済学を勉強する予定です。

● 未来のことを表すとき、will や be going to を使います。「(これから) ～します、～するでしょう」と言う場合は、will を使います。

主語	will＋動詞の原形	その他の情報	意味
I	**will** buy	a new smartphone tomorrow.	私は明日、新しいスマートフォンを買います。
Kevin	**will** sing	at the concert tonight.	ケビンは今夜コンサートで歌うでしょう。

● すでに決まっている予定や確実に起こりそうなことを表す場合は、be going to を使います。

主語	be動詞＋going to ＋動詞の原形	その他の情報	意味
We	**are going to** visit	Kamakura this weekend.	私たちは今週末、鎌倉を訪れる予定です。
Yuki	**is going to** leave	for Quebec tonight.	ユキは今夜ケベックに向けて出発する予定です。

● 否定文は、will または be 動詞の後ろに not をつけます。

I **will not** [**won't**] apply for the job.
私はその仕事に応募しません。

It **is not going to** rain this afternoon.
今日の午後、雨は降らないでしょう。

● 疑問文は、主語の前に will または be 動詞を置きます。

Will Lisa come to Japan next year?
リサは来年日本に来ますか。

Are you **going to** see Tom tomorrow?
あなたは明日トムに会いますか。

Grammar Checking

A (　　) 内から正しいほうの選択肢を選び、文を完成させましょう。 CheckLink

1. (**a.** I'll **b.** I'll going to) call you later.
2. We're (**a.** going to there **b.** going to go there) by taxi.
3. He didn't take the test, so he (**a.** won't **b.** not going to) pass the class.
4. What (**a.** will you **b.** are you going) to do today?
5. We'll (**a.** going to have **b.** have) pasta for dinner.
6. How long (**a.** you will **b.** will you) stay in Okinawa?
7. I'm (**a.** not going to **b.** going not to) eat junk food anymore.
8. (**a.** I won't be **b.** I'm not going to) late. I promise.

B 1～4の空所には will か won't を入れ、5～8の空所には be going to を適切な形に変えて入れ、文を完成させましょう。

1. Don't drink coffee before bed. You ______________ sleep.
2. There was a train accident. I ______________ be late for class.
3. You don't need your umbrella today. It ______________ rain.
4. Bye, Jane. I ______________ call you around 9:00.
5. I'm tired. I ____________________ take a rest.
6. I saw this movie before, but I didn't like it. I ____________________ watch it again.
7. Justin is in L.A. for the weekend. He ________________________ see some friends.
8. Joe and Sue are both sick. They ______________________ go to Amy's party.

Reading ● *Travelog — Old Quebec (Vieux Québec)*

エミの旅行日記を読み、紹介されている順に写真a～cに番号を振りましょう。

CheckLink  DL 66  CD 66

Today, I'm going to look inside the Château Frontenac. It's a 611-room hotel on a hill that opened in 1893. Then I'll take a carriage ride around Old Quebec. I'm also going to return to Artist Alley and buy a few pictures. I hope I'll be able to talk to some of the artists there, too.

Note: carriage ride「馬車」

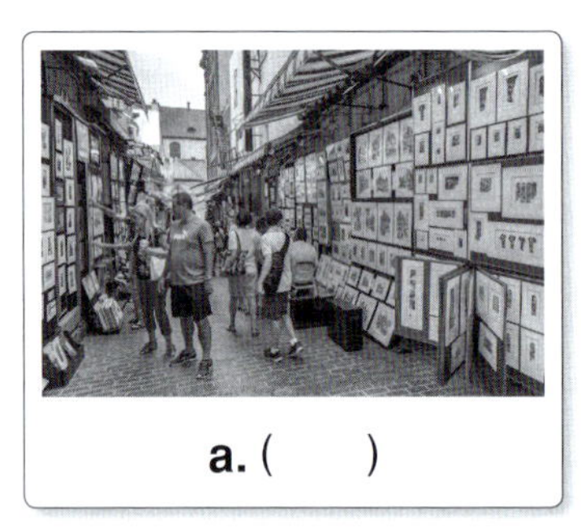

a. (　　)

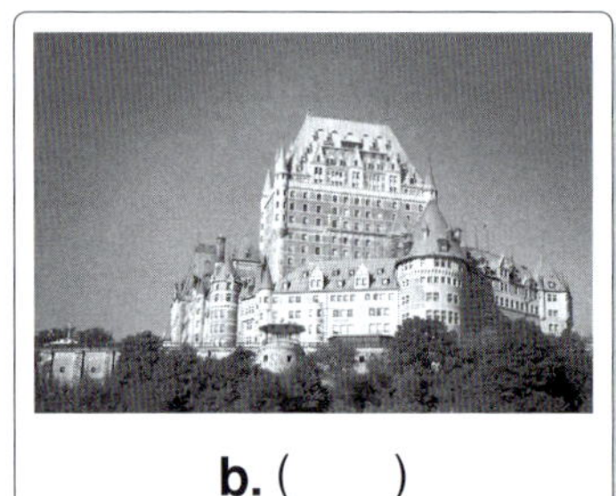

b. (　　)

c. (　　)

Mission ! 2. あなた自身について書いてみよう！

Aのセリフの空所にあなた自身の情報を書き込んで、会話を完成させましょう（未来形を使いましょう）。

DL 67 CD 67

A: What are you going to do on the weekend?

B: Well, I'm going to go to a concert on Saturday. On Sunday, I think I'll take a walk in the park. What are your plans?

A: On Saturday, ______________________________.

On Sunday, I think ______________________________.

Hints go shopping「買い物に行く」 visit a museum「美術館を訪れる」 play soccer「サッカーをする」 stay home and relax「家でくつろぐ」 practice the violin「バイオリンを練習する」 clean my room「部屋を掃除する」 buy some new clothes「新しい服を買う」

Unit 12 Florida Sunshine

Mission !
- 期間をたずねよう
- 現在完了形を使った英文に慣れよう

Getting Ready

リョウはマイアミ・ビーチにやってきました。

How long have you had her?
a
b
c
d

A 1～4を表すイラストを上のa～dから選びましょう。

CheckLink DL 68 CD 68

1. lifeguard (　　)　**2.** seashell (　　)　**3.** toy (　　)　**4.** trash can (　　)

B イラストを見ながら1～4の英文を聞きましょう。イラストと合っていればT、合っていなければFを選びましょう。

CheckLink DL 69 CD 69

1. T / F　**2.** T / F　**3.** T / F　**4.** T / F

Conversation ● *Ryo's Date with Isabelle*

ビーチでリラックスしていたリョウに、１匹の犬が飛びついてきました。

A 会話を聞いて、聞き取った内容と合っているほうの選択肢を選びましょう。

CheckLink　DL 70　CD 70

1. Isabelle is the (**a.** dog's　**b.** jogger's) name.

2. The jogger has had her dog for about (**a.** six months　**b.** one year).

3. Ryo (**a.** has a big dog　**b.** doesn't have a dog).

4. Ryo will go to a (**a.** coffee shop　**b.** park) with the jogger and her dog.

B もう一度会話を聞いて、空所を埋めましょう。

Jogger: Isabelle! Come here! *(to Ryo)* I'm so sorry.

Ryo: It's OK. I think I've ([1]　　　　　　　) a new friend. She's beautiful. **How long have you had her?**

Jogger: Since I moved to Miami, so, about a year. Do you have a dog?

Ryo: No, but ([2]　　　　　　　) always wanted a big dog like yours.

Jogger: I've always ([3]　　　　　　　) big dogs, too. Hey, have you ([4]　　　　　　　) lunch?

Ryo: No, I ([5]　　　　　　　).

Jogger: Well, Isabelle and I are going to a dog café. Do you want to come?

Ryo: Yes. Thank you. I've never ([6]　　　　　　　) to a dog café before.

Mission ! 1. セリフを言ってみよう！

音声を聞いて、下のセリフを確認しましょう。その後で、前のページのイラストを見ながら吹き出しのセリフを言ってみましょう。　DL 71　CD 71

How long have you had her?

How long ~ ?で、「どのくらい長く～していますか」とたずねることができます。また、「ペットを飼う」と言うとき、動詞はhaveを使います。

Breaking Down the Grammar ● 現在完了形

The last train **has left.**

終電が行ってしまいました。

● 現在完了形は、今までに経験したこと（経験）や、ずっと続けていること（継続）、やり終えたこと（完了）などについて述べるときに使います。現在完了形の文は、主語の後に「have / has ＋ 動詞の過去分詞形」を使います。

	主語	have / has ＋過去分詞	その他の情報	意味
経験	I	**have seen**	a UFO before.	私は以前UFOを見たことがあります。
継続	We	**have lived**	in Nagoya for 10 years.	私たちは名古屋に10年間住んでいます。
完了	John	**has finished**	making cookies.	ジョンはクッキーを作り終えました。

▶動詞の過去分詞は、巻末の「不規則変化動詞一覧」でチェックしましょう。

● 否定文は、have / has の後ろに not や never をつけます。

I **haven't** [**have not**] **finished** my homework. 私は宿題を終えていません。

Ken **has never been** to USJ.
ケンは USJ（ユニバーサル・スタジオ・ジャパン）に一度も行ったことがありません。

● 疑問文は、主語の前に have / has を置きます。

Have you **had** dinner?
あなたは夕食を食べましたか。

Has Jane ever **visited** Tokyo?
ジェーンは今までに東京を訪れたことがありますか。

▶「今までに〜したことがありますか」とたずねる場合、現在完了形と一緒にeverを使います。

Grammar Checking

A (　　) 内から正しいほうの選択肢を選び、文を完成させましょう。 CheckLink

1. Maki has (**a.** gone　**b.** went) to the convenience store.
2. It has (**a.** been snowed　**b.** snowed) almost every day this week.
3. (**a.** Had you have　**b.** Have you had) lunch?
4. Have (**a.** you ever　**b.** ever you) been to Hokkaido?
5. Kaori has (**a.** her textbook lost　**b.** lost her textbook).
6. (**a.** Has　**b.** Have) anyone seen my hat?
7. Mark (**a.** has never　**b.** hasn't never) gone snowboarding.
8. I have (**a.** golf played　**b.** played golf) before, but only once.

B 空所に入る動詞を枠内から選び、現在完了形にして書き入れましょう。

buy (買う)	forget (忘れる)	~~go (行く)~~	ride (乗る)
see (見る)	stop (止まる)	tell (教える)	

1. **A:** Where's Tim?　**B:** He ___has___ ___gone___ to the bank.
2. **A:** Look! Don and Karen ________ ________ a new car.　**B:** It's nice!
3. **A:** I'm looking for my keys. ________ you ________ them?
   B: No, I haven't.
4. **A:** Does Alex know about the party?　**B:** No, no one ________ ________ him.
5. **A:** ________ you ever ________ a horse?　**B:** Yes, once. It was really fun!
6. **A:** ________ it ________ raining?　**B:** No, it's still raining hard.
7. **A:** I know that guy, but I ________ ________ his name.
   B: That's Ed Cox.

Reading ● *Travelog — Been There, Done That*

リョウの旅行日記を読み、紹介されている順に写真a～cに番号を振りましょう。

CheckLink DL 72 CD 72

I've been in Florida for two days. Miami Beach has about 30 unique lifeguard towers. I've taken pictures of all of them! I've also visited the Kennedy Space Center. I enjoyed an airboat tour of the Florida Everglades, too. I even saw an alligator. I haven't been to Disney World. I'll go there tomorrow.

Note: Florida Everglades「フロリダの大湿地帯」

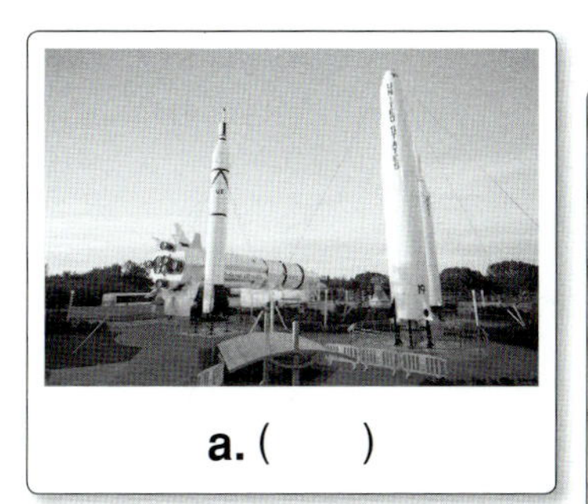

a. (　　)

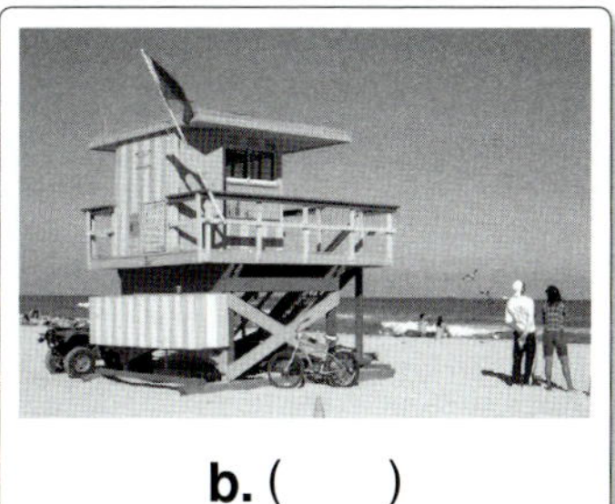

b. (　　)

c. (　　)

Mission ! 2. あなた自身について書いてみよう！

(　　) に正しい単語を入れて、現在完了形の疑問文を作りましょう。その後で、Bのセリフの空所にあなた自身の情報を書き込んで、会話を完成させましょう。

DL 73 CD 73

A: I've been to Tokyo Disneyland three times. (　　　　　　) you ever been there?

B: ______________________________. What other fun places (　　　　　　) you (　　　　　　) to?

A: Well, I've been to Huis Ten Bosch in Nagasaki and Ueno Zoo in Tokyo. How about you?

B: I ______________________________ and ______________________________.

Unit 13

A Taste of P.E.I.

Mission !
- おすすめについて話そう
- 比較級・最上級を使った英文に慣れよう

Getting Ready

エミは、プリンスエドワード島 (P.E.I.) で食事を楽しんでいます。

Does P.E.I. have the best seafood?
a
b
c
d

A 1～4を表すイラストを上のa～dから選びましょう。

CheckLink DL 74 CD 74

1. beans (　　)　**2.** French fries (　　)　**3.** lobster (　　)　**4.** tart (　　)

B イラストを見ながら1～4の英文を聞きましょう。イラストと合っていればT、合っていなければFを選びましょう。

CheckLink DL 75 CD 75

1. T / F　**2.** T / F　**3.** T / F　**4.** T / F

Conversation　● *A Lobster Tale*

エミは、シーフードについてウェイターと話しています。

A 会話を聞いて、聞き取った内容と合っているほうの選択肢を選びましょう。

CheckLink　DL 76　CD 76

1. Emi ordered the (**a.** lobster　**b.** seafood) special.
2. The waiter says that P.E.I. has the (**a.** freshest　**b.** juiciest) seafood.
3. The largest lobsters weigh (**a.** 8　**b.** 18) kilograms.
4. Soft shell lobsters are (**a.** cheaper　**b.** more expensive) than hard shell lobsters.

B もう一度会話を聞いて、空所を埋めましょう。

Waiter: Here's your seafood special. Enjoy your meal.
Emi: Thank you. **Does P.E.I. have the best seafood?**
Waiter: Yes, it's the ([1]　　　　　　　) *and* the ([2]　　　　　　　) delicious.
Emi: Really?
Waiter: Well, we think it is. Ha ha ha!
Emi: Are all lobsters the same?
Waiter: Oh, no. Soft shell lobsters have ([3]　　　　　　　), softer and ([4]　　　　　　　) meat ([5]　　　　　　　) hard shell lobsters. They're also a little ([6]　　　　　　　). Some lobsters grow to be more than 120 cm long and weigh 18 kg.
Emi: Woah! That sounds scary!

Notes: soft shell lobster「殻の柔らかいロブスター」　hard shell lobster「殻の硬いロブスター」

1. セリフを言ってみよう！

音声を聞いて、下のセリフを確認しましょう。その後で、前のページのイラストを見ながら吹き出しのセリフを言ってみましょう。　DL 77　CD 77

> ***Does P.E.I. have the best seafood?***

Yes/Noで答えられる疑問文は通常、文末のイントネーションを上げて発音します。疑問詞から始まる疑問文は、文末のイントネーションを下げて発音します。

Salad is **healthier than** French fries.

サラダはフライドポテトよりも健康的です。

● 2 つのものを比べて「A は B より～だ」と言うときは、比較級を使います。

主語＋動詞	比較級	than＋比較対象	意味
My room is	small**er**	than yours.	私の部屋はあなたの部屋よりも狭いです。
Soccer is	**more** popular	than baseball in this country.	この国では野球よりもサッカーのほうが人気があります。
I have	a **better** idea	than yours.	私はあなたのものよりもよいアイディアをもっています。

● 3 つ以上のものを比べて「A が一番～だ」と言うときは、最上級を使います。

主語＋動詞	最上級	範囲を表す語句	意味
Tim is	**the** young**est**	of the five members.	ティムは 5 人のメンバーの中で一番若いです。
This is	**the most** expensive	watch in this shop.	これはこの店で一番高価な時計です。
That was	**the worst** movie	I've ever seen.	その映画は私が今まで観た中で最悪でした。

Grammar Checking

A (　　) 内から正しいほうの選択肢を選び、文を完成させましょう。 CheckLink

1. Toronto is (**a.** more big　**b.** bigger) than Vancouver.
2. Chicken is (**a.** cheaper　**b.** more cheaper) than beef.
3. The cheetah is (**a.** the most quickly　**b.** the fastest) land animal on earth.
4. What are (**a.** the most　**b.** more than) popular sports in your country?
5. Michael is a (**a.** more good　**b.** better) singer than Bruce.
6. This is the (**a.** worst　**b.** worse) steak I have ever eaten!
7. A meter is (**a.** a yard longer than　**b.** longer than a yard).
8. What's the (**a.** thing most expensive　**b.** most expensive thing) you have?

B 例のように [　　] 内の語句を使い、2、3は比較級の文、4、5は最上級の文を作りましょう。

1. Laura is 19. Liz is 18.
   [**old**] *Laura is older than Liz.*
2. Mari is 160 cm tall. Saki is 155 cm tall.
   [**tall**] ______________________________
3. Ben weighs 60 kg. Gary weighs 70 kg.
   [**heavy**] ______________________________
4. Mt. Fuji is 3,776 m, Mt. McKinley is 6,190 m, and Mt. Everest is 8,848 m.
   [**high mountain**]
   ______________________________ in the world.
5. Canada is 9,984,000 km^2, the U.S. is 9,630,000 km^2, and Russia is 17,100,000 km^2.
   [**big country**]
   ______________________________ in the world.

Reading ● *Travelog — Small Is Beautiful*

エミの旅行日記を読み、紹介されている順に写真a～cに番号を振りましょう。

CheckLink DL 78 

Prince Edward Island, or P.E.I., is the smallest province in Canada. It is much smaller than Shikoku, and its biggest city, Charlottetown, has only about 40,000 people. One of the most famous attractions in P.E.I. is Green Gables House. It is home to the red-haired character Anne of Green Gables. I bought a cute Anne doll. I also visited the oldest lighthouse in P.E.I.

Notes: province「州」 Anne of Green Gables「赤毛のアン」

a. (　　)

b. (　　)

c. (　　)

Mission ! 2. あなた自身について書いてみよう！

Bのセリフの空所にあなた自身の意見を書き込んで、会話を完成させましょう。
(　　) には big city / small town のいずれかを書き入れましょう。

DL 79 CD 79

A: In the future, do you want to live in a big city or a small town?

B: A (　　　　　　　　　　).

A: Why?

B: A (　　　　　　　　　　) is ______________ and ______________ than a (　　　　　　　　　　). It's ______________, too.

Hints quiet / noisy「静かな／騒がしい」 relaxing / stressful「くつろげる／ストレスが多い」 safe / dangerous「安全な／危険な」 exciting / boring「ワクワクする／つまらない」

N.Y.C. — The Big Apple

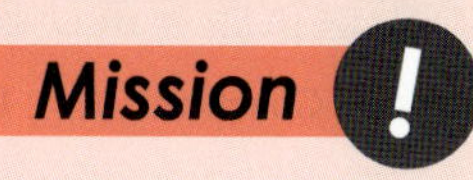

- 相手をほめよう
- 助動詞を使った英文に慣れよう

Getting Ready

リョウは、ニューヨークでブロードウェイ・ミュージカルを楽しんでいます。

A 1～4を表すイラストを上のa～dから選びましょう。

CheckLink　DL 80　CD 80

1. actors (　　)　**2.** audience (　　)　**3.** stage (　　)　**4.** box seat (　　)

B イラストを見ながら1～4の英文を聞きましょう。イラストと合っていればT、合っていなければFを選びましょう。

CheckLink　DL 81　CD 81

1. T / F　**2.** T / F　**3.** T / F　**4.** T / F

Conversation ● *Bravos from Ryo*

終演後、リョウは隣の席に座っていた女性と話をしています。

A 会話を聞いて、聞き取った内容と合っているほうの選択肢を選びましょう。

CheckLink DL 82 CD 82

1. Ryo says that Anna can sing and (**a.** act **b.** dance) well.
2. The lady thinks Ryo should wait for Anna (**a.** in the lobby **b.** outside).
3. Anna will probably leave the theater in about (**a.** 30 **b.** 60) minutes.
4. Ryo (**a.** has time **b.** doesn't have time) to wait for Anna.

B もう一度会話を聞いて、空所を埋めましょう。

Ryo: Bravo! Bravo!
Lady: You really liked the show, didn't you?
Ryo: Yes, especially Anna. **She can sing and dance very well.** And she's so...
Lady: ...beautiful?
Ryo: Yes, beautiful. I'm so lucky I ([1]) see the show ... and her.
Lady: You ([2]) wait for her outside. She ([3]) sign autographs. You ([4]) even be able to take a picture with her.
Ryo: Really?
Lady: Yes, really. You ([5]) to wait for about an hour, though.
Ryo: Oh, I don't mind waiting. Thank you so much!
Lady: Oh, you ([6]) have to thank me. Now go. And good luck!

Note: sign autographs「サインする」

Mission ! 1. セリフを言ってみよう！

音声を聞いて、下のセリフを確認しましょう。その後で、前のページのイラストを見ながら吹き出しのセリフを言ってみましょう。 DL 83 CD 83

She can sing and dance very well.

Sheのshは、静かにしてほしいときに「シー！」と言うときと似ていて、唇をすぼめて発音します。singのsは日本語の「い」の口の形で「スー」と息を吐きながら発音します。

Breaking Down the Grammar ●助動詞

基本
例文

We might go to see the opera this weekend.
私たちは今週末、オペラを見に行くかもしれません。

●助動詞には、動詞に意味をつけ加える役割があります。

助動詞	例文
can / could 「～できる・できた」	Peter **can / could** ski well. ピーターは上手にスキーを滑ることができます（できました）。
may / might 「～かもしれない」	Aki **may / might** know your brother. アキはあなたのお兄さんを知っているかもしれません。
should 「～すべき」	You **should** wear a warm sweater today. あなたは今日、暖かいセーターを着るべきです。
must 「～しなければならない」	You **must** take off your shoes here. あなたはここでは靴を脱がなければなりません。
have to 「～しなければならない」	We **have to** be home by 7:00. 私たちは7時までに帰宅しなければなりません。

●否定文は、助動詞の後ろに not をつけます。have to の場合は動詞の前に don't / doesn't / didn't をつけます。

We **could not** [**couldn't**] answer the question.
私たちはその問題に答えられませんでした。

You **don't have to** wait for me.
あなたは私を待っている（待つ）必要はありません。

●疑問文は、主語の前に助動詞を置きます。have to の場合は主語の前に Do / Does / Did をつけます。

Can you come to the concert tonight?
あなたは今晩コンサートに来られますか。

Did Ben **have to** work last night?
ベンは昨晩働かなければならなかったですか。

It can speak six languages!

Grammar Checking

A (　　) 内から正しいほうの選択肢を選び、文を完成させましょう。　CheckLink

1. Can you (**a.** speak　**b.** speaking) Chinese?
2. These grapes are delicious.　You (**a.** has to　**b.** should) try some.
3. I (**a.** have to　**b.** could) go to class.　It starts in five minutes.
4. We (**a.** can't　**b.** couldn't) hear the teacher.　He spoke softly.
5. Michelle (**a.** can　**b.** might) go to the party.　She's not sure.
6. Take your time.　You (**a.** don't have to　**b.** must) hurry.
7. How long does she (**a.** has to　**b.** have to) work tonight?
8. Buses ONLY!　Cars (**a.** must not　**b.** don't have to) park here.

B (　　) 内の語句を並べ替えて、Aに対する応答を完成させましょう。

1. **A:** It's a beautiful clear night.　(stars / see / we / many / can)

   B: Yes, it is. ______________________________.

2. **A:** Did you read the sign?　(must / glasses / safety / everyone / wear)

   B: Yes.　It says, "______________________________."

3. **A:** Jin is always late for school.　(earlier / he / home / leave / should)

   B: ______________________________.

4. **A:** The zoo isn't crowded today.　(wait / to / don't / we / have)

   B: Yay! ______________________________ to enter.

5. **A:** What are you going to do tonight?　(movie / a / go / might / to / I)

   B: ______________________________.

Reading　Travelog — New York on the Cheap

リョウの旅行日記を読み、紹介されている順に写真a～cに番号を振りましょう。

CheckLink　DL 84　CD 84

New York is expensive, but you don't have to spend any money to do some really cool things. For example, you can walk across the Brooklyn Bridge. It took me about an hour. From the bridge, I could see beautiful views of Manhattan and the Statue of Liberty. Central Park is a great place to visit during the day, and Times Square is really exciting, especially at night.

a. (　　)

b. (　　)

c. (　　)

Mission ! 2. あなた自身について書いてみよう！

Aのセリフの空所にあなた自身の情報を書き込んで、会話を完成させましょう。

DL 85　CD 85

A: Are you busy next week? What are you going to do?

B: I have to write a report. I should buy some food at the supermarket, too. And I might have dinner with a friend. Are you busy?

A: Well, I have to ______________________________. I should also ______________________________. And I may ______________________________.

Hints go to the doctor「医者に行く」　finish an assignment「宿題を終える」　play tennis「テニスをする」　go to a friend's house「友達の家に行く」

Unit 15

Niagara Falls

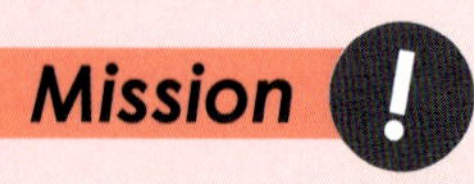
Mission !

- 思い出について話そう
- 受動態を使った英文に慣れよう

Getting Ready

エミとリョウは、ついにカナダのナイアガラの滝で落ち合いました。

When was this photo taken?
a
b
c
d

A 1～4を表すイラストを上のa～dから選びましょう。

CheckLink　DL 86　CD 86

1. cheek (　　)　**2.** rainbow (　　)　**3.** snapshot (　　)　**4.** waterfall (　　)

B イラストを見ながら1～4の英文を聞きましょう。イラストと合っていればT、合っていなければFを選びましょう。

CheckLink　DL 87　CD 87

1. T / F　**2.** T / F　**3.** T / F　**4.** T / F

Conversation ● *Emi and Ryo Meet Mary and Walt*

仲の良さそうな老夫婦が、エミとリョウに話しかけてきました。

A 会話を聞いて、聞き取った内容と合っているほうの選択肢を選びましょう。

CheckLink DL 88 CD 88

1. Ryo tells Mary that he and Emi are (**a.** best **b.** just) friends.
2. Niagara Falls is called the (**a.** honeymoon **b.** wedding) capital of the world.
3. Mary and Walt were married (**a.** 50 **b.** 60) years ago.
4. The message on the back of the photo was written by (**a.** Mary **b.** Walt).

B もう一度会話を聞いて、空所を埋めましょう。

Mary: Are you two here on your honeymoon?
Ryo: Ha ha ha! No, we're just friends.
Mary: Niagara Falls is ([1]) the honeymoon capital of the world.
Walt: Mary and I came here on our honeymoon. Here's a snapshot.
Emi: **When was this photo taken?**
Walt: Well, we were ([2]) 60 years ago. This town was still small.
Mary: Then new hotels were ([3]), new restaurants were ([4])…
Ryo: …and new tourist attractions were ([5])?
Mary: Right. Tell them what's ([6]) on the back of the photo, Walt.
Walt: It says, "I'll love you forever, Mary. Love Walt."
Emi: Ohhhh, that's so romantic!

Notes: the honeymoon capital of the world「ハネムーンの聖地」 tourist attractions「観光名所」

Mission ! 1. セリフを言ってみよう！

音声を聞いて、下のセリフを確認しましょう。その後で、前のページのイラストを見ながら吹き出しのセリフを言ってみましょう。 DL 89 CD 89

> ***When was this photo taken?***

photoの発音は「フォト」ではなく「フォウトゥ [fóutou]」となります。同じ意味の単語であるphotographの発音は「フォウタグラフ [fóutəgræf]」です。

Breaking Down the Grammar ● 受動態

基本
例文

The idols were cheered by their fans.
そのアイドルたちはファンから声援を受けました。

●受動態（[人やものが] ～される／された）の文を作るときは、主語の後に「be動詞＋過去分詞」を続けます。過去分詞には「～される／された」という意味があります。

主語	be動詞＋過去分詞	その他の情報	意味
Fresh vegetables	**are sold**	in this store.	この店では新鮮な野菜が売られています。
This pie	**was made**	by my grandmother.	このパイは私の祖母によって作られました。
Many houses	**were damaged**	in the typhoon.	その台風で多くの家が被害を受けました。

▶「～によって」と動作の主体となる人を表すときには、by ～ をつけます。by ～ は、動作の主体が明らかである場合は省略されます。また、by以外の前置詞（for / as / of / inなど）が来る場合もあります。

●否定文を作るときは、be動詞の後ろにnotをつけます。

This table **isn't made** of wood. このテーブルは木製ではありません。

Eating and drinking **are not allowed** in this room.
この部屋の中では飲食は禁止されています。

●疑問文を作るときは、主語の前にbe動詞を置きます。

Is this song **sung** by the Beatles?
この歌はビートルズによって歌われていますか。

Was this temple **built** 100 years ago?
この寺は100年前に建てられましたか。

It's called a selfie stick.

Grammar Checking

A (　　) 内から正しいほうの選択肢を選び、文を完成させましょう。 CheckLink

1. The hotel rooms are (**a.** cleaning **b.** cleaned) every day.
2. This house (**a.** is **b.** was) built 150 years ago.
3. Spanish is (**a.** spoke **b.** spoken) in Mexico.
4. "Baby" is (**a.** song **b.** sung) by Justin Bieber.
5. These sketches were all (**a.** drawn **b.** drew) by Emi.
6. Are (**a.** pineapples grown **b.** grown pineapples) in Okinawa?
7. (**a.** Tom was hit by a car **b.** A car was hit Tom) yesterday.
8. Where (**a.** were these photos taken **b.** these photos were taken)?

B 例にならって、文を受動態に書き換えましょう。

1. Someone locks the door at 8 p.m.

   The door is locked at 8 p.m.

2. People sell old records and CDs here.

   ____

3. Do people make this wine in France?

   ____

4. Someone stole Aki's bicycle last night.

   ____

5. People wore these clothes in the 1970s.

   ____

6. Where did someone take this picture?

   ____

Reading　Travelog — Emi's Day with Ryo

エミの旅行日記を読み、紹介されている順に写真a〜cに番号を振りましょう。

CheckLink　DL 90　CD 90

Today, I met Ryo on the Canadian side of Niagara Falls. We rode this Ferris wheel. It's called Niagara SkyWheel. From the top, we had a great view of the falls. After that, we joined a tour and were taken near the falls in a boat. It was thrilling ... and WET! We had dinner in the Skylon Tower with our new friends Mary and Walt.

Note: Ferris wheel「観覧車」

a. (　　)

b. (　　)

c. (　　)

Mission !　2. あなた自身について書いてみよう！

(　　) に、write / sing のいずれかを過去分詞形にして入れましょう。その後、A のセリフの空所にあなた自身の情報を書き込んで、会話を完成させましょう。

DL 91　CD 91

A: What's your favorite book?

B: It's *Botchan*. It was (　　　　　　) by Soseki Natsume. What's your favorite song?

A: My favorite song is "____________________." It's (　　　　　　) by ____________________.

会話表現 & 基本例文一覧

Mission! 1 で学習した会話表現と、Breaking Down the Grammar の基本例文の一覧です。

Unit 1 ［ホテルにチェックインする／ be 動詞］	
□ チェックインをお願いします。	I'm here to check in.
□ バンクーバーは美しい街です。	Vancouver is a beautiful city.
Unit 2 ［行きたい場所を伝える／一般動詞の現在形］	
□ ダウンタウンに行きたいです。	I want to go downtown.
□ 私はサンフランシスコで働いています。	I work in San Francisco.
Unit 3 ［お礼を言う／代名詞］	
□ ご親切にありがとうございます。	That's very kind of you.
□ こちらは私の友人のリョウです。彼は日本から来ました。	This is my friend Ryo. He is from Japan.
Unit 4 ［探しているものを伝える／進行形］	
□ ヴィンテージ・ジーンズを探しています。	I'm looking for a pair of vintage jeans.
□ 私は今、オンラインゲームをしています。	I am playing an online game now.
Unit 5 ［お願いをする／時と場所を表す前置詞］	
□ ちょっと待ってください。	Please wait for a minute.
□ 私のおじはロサンゼルスに住んでいます。	My uncle lives in Los Angeles.

Unit 6 ［単位の違いを理解する／可算名詞・不可算名詞］	
□ 1ガロンは1リットルくらいですか。	Is a gallon about one liter?
□ 私は朝食にバナナ2本と紅茶1杯をとります。	I have two bananas and a cup of tea for breakfast.
Unit 7 ［感想を述べる／一般動詞の過去形］	
□ はい、満喫しました。	Yes, I enjoyed every minute!
□ 私たちは先週末、フリーマーケットを訪れました。	We visited the flea market last weekend.
Unit 8 ［会話を続ける／疑問詞］	
□ あなたはどうですか。	How about you?
□ あなたはどこに住んでいますか。	Where do you live?
Unit 9 ［注文する／接続詞］	
□ 私はフルーツが好きなので、バナナチョコレートがほしいです。	I like fruit, so I want Banana Chocolate.
□ 私はピアノを持っていますが、それを演奏しません。	I have a piano, but I don’t play it.
Unit 10 ［やりたいことを伝える／動名詞・不定詞］	
□ ミュージシャンに会いたいです。	I hope to meet some musicians.
□ ジムは一晩中踊り続けました。	Jim kept dancing all night long.

Unit 11 [滞在日数を伝える／未来形]	
□ 2、3日滞在します。	I'll stay for two or three days.
□ 私は大学で経済学を勉強する予定です。	I am going to study economics in college.
Unit 12 [期間をたずねる／現在完了形]	
□ どのくらい彼女を飼っていますか。	How long have you had her?
□ 終電が行ってしまいました。	The last train has left.
Unit 13 [おすすめについて話す／比較級・最上級]	
□ P.E.I. のシーフードは最高ですか。	Does P.E.I. have the best seafood?
□ サラダはフライドポテトよりも健康的です。	Salad is healthier than French fries.
Unit 14 [ほめる／助動詞]	
□ 彼女はとても上手に歌って踊れます。	She can sing and dance very well.
□ 私たちは今週末、オペラを見に行くかもしれません。	We might go to see the opera this weekend.
Unit 15 [思い出を話す／受動態]	
□ この写真はいつ撮られたんですか。	When was this photo taken?
□ そのアイドルたちはファンから声援を受けました。	The idols were cheered by their fans.

不規則変化動詞一覧

現在形	過去形	過去分詞形
□ be「～である」	was / were	been
□ bring「持っていく」	brought	brought
□ buy「買う」	bought	bought
□ catch「捕まえる」	caught	caught
□ come「来る」	came	come
□ do「する」	did	done
□ drink「飲む」	drank	drunk
□ draw「描く」	drew	drawn
□ eat「食べる」	ate	eaten
□ fall「落ちる」	fell	fallen
□ find「見つける」	found	found
□ forget「忘れる」	forgot	forgot / forgotten
□ get「得る」	got	got / gotten
□ give「与える」	gave	given
□ go「行く」	went	gone
□ have「持つ」	had	had
□ hear「聞く」	heard	heard
□ know「知る」	knew	known
□ leave「去る」	left	left
□ lose「失う」	lost	lost
□ make「作る」	made	made
□ meet「会う」	met	met
□ put「置く」	put	put
□ read「読む」	read	read
□ run「走る」	ran	run
□ say「言う」	said	said
□ see「見る」	saw	seen
□ sell「売る」	sold	sold
□ send「送る」	sent	sent
□ sing「歌う」	sang	sung
□ take「とる」	took	taken
□ tell「話す」	told	told
□ write「書く」	wrote	written

ここからはがして下さい

このシールをはがすと
CheckLink 利用のための
「教科書固有番号」が
記載されています。

一度はがすと元に戻すことは
できませんのでご注意下さい。

4070 English Missions!
Starter

CheckLink

本書にはCD（別売）があります

English Missions! Starter

ミッション型 大学英語の総合演習：入門編

2019年1月20日　初版第1刷発行
2024年2月20日　初版第9刷発行

著　者　Robert Hickling
　　　　臼倉美里

発行者　福岡正人

発行所　株式会社　金星堂

（〒101-0051）東京都千代田区神田神保町3-21
Tel.（03）3263-3828（営業部）
（03）3263-3997（編集部）
Fax（03）3263-0716
https://www.kinsei-do.co.jp

編集担当　西田 碧　　Printed in Japan

印刷所・製本所／萩原印刷株式会社

本書の無断複製・複写は著作権法上での例外を除き禁じられています。
本書を代行業者等の第三者に依頼してスキャンやデジタル化することは、たとえ個人や家庭内での利用であっても認められておりません。
落丁・乱丁本はお取り替えいたします。

ISBN978-4-7647-4070-9　C1082